THE BIOGRAPHY OF BLIND SURFER DEREK RABELO
BEYOND THESE EYES
WRITTEN WITH **LYNN GOLDSMITH**

Ark House Press
PO Box 1722, Port Orchard, WA 98366 USA
PO Box 1321, Mona Vale NSW 1660 Australia
PO Box 318 334, West Harbour, Auckland 0661 New Zealand
arkhousepress.com

© 2019 Ark House Press
All rights reserved. No part of this publication may be reproduced, stored in a retrieval system or transmitted in any form or by any means electronic, mechanical, photocopying, recording or otherwise without the prior written permission of the publisher.

Cataloguing in Publication Data:
Title: Beyond These Eyes: The Biography of Blind Surfer Derek Rabelo
ISBN: 9780648458586 (pbk.) 978-0-6485077-9-6 (ebk)
Subjects: Biography, Christian
Other Authors/Contributors: Rabelo, Derek; Goldsmith, Lynn

Design and layout by initiateagency.com

CONTENTS

Foreword with Tom Carroll   vii
Prologue   xiii

Chapter 1.   My Destiny – Amazing Where I Am Now!   1
Chapter 2.   I Came Into This World Screaming!   8
Chapter 3.   Love Conquers All   21
Chapter 4.   School – Oh Happy Days!   30
Chapter 5.   Conquering The Impossible   45
Chapter 6.   My Goal – College Or Surf?   57
Chapter 7.   Hawaii – My Pipeline Dream   62
Chapter 8.   A Young Star Is Born   75
Chapter 9.   My Time 'Down Under'   86
Chapter 10.   Love Is In The Air   98
Chapter 11.   The Wedding Of The Year…   114
Chapter 12.   Travel Time   129
Chapter 13.   What Keeps Me Going In Life   139
Chapter 14.   My Dog - My Precious Companion!   149
Chapter 15.   The Rush Of Riding Big Waves   158
Chapter 16.   My Destiny – Nazaré And Jaws   170

Epilogue   190
Testimonials   194
About The Author   218

FOREWORD

WITH TOM CARROLL

I first met Derek Rabelo when a friend who was filming a documentary introduced me to him. That was the start of a beautiful friendship with an extraordinary man.

When I first walked out to surf with Derek at North Narrabeen in Sydney, I knew he couldn't see. It was one thing to meet him, but another to actually experience riding the waves with him. Honestly, I didn't know what to think or what to expect. How could this guy ride the waves blind? Fortunately, his father was with him, making some particular noises so he could understand the ocean. This was something they had developed between them. I definitely didn't understand it.

There was a shore break waist high and after that came some unbroken waves. There was deep water, with a current sucking us out into a crowded lineup of surfers. This was an aggressive lineup. It's not much fun when a beach is crowded and guarded by the locals. It's a tough place to be – even when you can see.

I was fiddling with a GoPro camera to get myself ready so I could capture this moment with Derek. I knew it was very special. I watched him as he jumped forward ahead of me. I was watching where he was going. He went through the shore break and paddled straight. Where was he going? I was trying to figure it out. He was paddling, but he couldn't see! How was this happening? I tried to put myself in his shoes. I could hear his father making sounds, but then I lost him. I guess he knew what he was doing, but was he insane?

I was paddling out with the camera, but he had taken off on a one and a half meter swell. I assumed he was going to take his time to get a wave. Unfortunately, the camera was taking all my attention, so I couldn't see where he was. I was looking out at this set of waves coming in and Derek was taking off. His father was with him. Derek got this wave and I thought, *'Oh no, he got this wave.'*

There were many people paddling nearby, but those people didn't know he was blind. On this wave, he rode it for 100 metres down the sand bar. I took off on the next wave to try and catch him, but where did he go? So where does Derek think he is when he is in the water? If I can't find him, how does he find where he is?

He had ridden the wave as far as he could go. At that point, I was completely blown away. He hadn't hit anyone, thankfully. When I reached him, I said, "Derek are you okay?"

He said, "Yes." He turned around and paddled back out. He knew where he was in the ocean. He just duck dived under the waves and his senses were so acute. His brain has such a great capacity; everything is planned in his mind and beautiful to watch. At that point, I was moved to tears. I was blown away by his capacity to choose to really live. This was Derek Rabelo. From that day on, he's been non-stop and he has shown everyone he would continue to live like this on a daily basis.

At one stage, we were both in Hawaii at the same time. Derek called me and said, "Tom, I really want to surf Waimea Bay," and I thought, *'On no.'*

FOREWORD

But I regained my composure and said, "Let's go and surf." Derek needs a team of people to help him surf there, as well as anywhere where the waves are a decent size. It was completely insane to surf Waimea, but we were able to do it. We put on inflatable vests and did all the safety measures that were required. The scariest thing for him was getting in the water with the surf break. We had to really concentrate on keeping him safe and to help keep him concentrating. However, he was fine riding the actual waves.

When he went to Nazaré in Portugal, I was really concerned for him because it is potentially very dangerous. The team has to be strong around him and fortunately they have a great team there. Derek sent me a photo - I couldn't believe the way he was riding the waves! I didn't expect to see this. It was definitely the next level up, but classic.

Derek has that 'I won't let anything phase me' kind of attitude when it comes to putting everything on the line. His character just shines. That is unmistakable to anyone who comes in contact with him.

Derek is doing exactly what he is being called to do. He is answering the call from a greater place. Obviously he wants to send a message to help guide others on this journey we call life, which isn't always easy. It's full of challenges! I love the way Derek is using his disability, which we perceive as a massive challenge. He is showing us that this is only our perception of the way life is and that can be changed. That message shows up in Derek's daily movements, and for a person of his age on the planet in this life, it shows an immense depth of character. It shows suggestions from an older age: carrying wisdom that comes from an older wisdom. He is able to recognize this depth and carry it on in service to others. In being human, he hasn't skipped a beat.

This is consistent with the way Derek carries the message of living life to its fullest. He gives us this great gift and each time I see Derek, it is unmistakable.

A lot of us are caught up in the idea we don't need help – we can do it all on our own. Unfortunately it is our ego, which is always trying to transform us. One thing I admire about Derek is that he asks for help; he reaches out every time. He has to, and he is constantly reaching out. That is a wonderful message, one that maybe we miss when we have sight. One of the greatest messages is that we all need help. We might be blind to many things in our life that we need help with. Derek is a living, breathing alarm bell to this universal urge to connect, to help each other, or to reach out for help, even if it means that your hands are too full and you need someone to open a door.

Last time we met, we were having a salad in Avalon in Sydney. He was having trouble with the salad and was concentrating on what was going on in the bowl for him. Here was a person who was amazing; just noticing those small, everyday things and how he senses the world. The spirit remains very, very strong and he is a great example to us. This is the ultimate of the human experience. The spirit is always accessible and it's up to us what we want to do with it. There are always layers of choices along the way.

Derek has an incredible influence on people. My own experience is that is has opened my eyes to the fact that we are only limited by our own thinking and the restrictions we place on ourselves. It is really glaringly obvious when I'm with him and seeing what he does. You can sit there with him, talk with him and watch him having difficulty at times with what is in his bowl in front of him.

When he surfs Nazaré with a jet ski and deals with that, the impact is so powerful. There are no limits. It's so clear for him. When we see clarity at that level, it is super influential. We get caught in the fog of our limitations. I am so thankful for his clarity when I am surfing with him.

FOREWORD

It is astonishing that he can't see things – and I'm wresting with things and I can see! I think he likes the rush of the sensation of his body; the feeling of doing something in that power. For him just to be feeling it, not having the visual and the neuroplasticity of his brain and the human ability to adapt is really on fire inside Derek.

My own experience is that I have drawn in moments and I can never really tell when they will happen, but something happens through a charm and enthusiasm, sometimes by another person. It gets transformed to me. In that way, Derek was very powerful for me.

It wasn't until I took the action that any faith I was doing started to come about. Faith just came to me through a miraculous event. Faith for me comes by action. Seeing people who are challenged like Derek inspires us to take action. Faith in our own actions and faith in ourselves, and from there we inspire others as well.

To step out beyond ourselves, to take a risk and get out of the cotton wool that we wrap around ourselves. This is a constant. Nothing is certain, except death. What do we do with this time we are alive and have our senses is to cultivate faith. It is a practical movement towards action. Taking a risk, whether small or large, starts to cultivate faith. We make mistakes and we learn lessons through that. As long as we are involving others and taking a risk with ourselves and pushing our own limits! It doesn't have to be big; it can be small.

The ocean takes our minds, taking all our concentration, without our mind playing out any stories, because we get caught in the story of life. We are wonderful at making these stories to live by, so we get a relief from all the stories out in the ocean. What has happened to us, what we are in the world, who we are: all these things drop away. The storm clears away and the systems (nervous and endocrine) and the mind – it starts to recalibrate in such a vibrant fashion.

The veterans from combat experience relief and the body and the mind get a chance to recover and they get a relief from the constant tension that is felt deep in the body. From the tension of the trauma, the torment is able to be released in the cells, molecules and atoms. The ocean has limitless potential in healing the body and the mind. I am completely convinced of that. That is happening for Derek. He has been given this arena to flourish and be human.

I think any book, whether it is shared in audio form, or through simple book form – the written word is super important to get a message across in a more timeless way. Once books are placed into the public's hands, it lasts for a long time and can be passed on and shared. Derek's amazing story can be offered around to many different ways and forms and many different people. It spreads the message. His message is very powerful as a human being. He approaches everything, without his sensual world taken for granted. With all our senses together, when we see what Derek does and his journey and how he got to those places, and to see his mindset, is quite remarkable. This is very important to share. This book will give him an even bigger platform to speak from and be able to influence hundreds of thousands of additional people.

Tom Carroll
Former two-time surfing world champion

PROLOGUE

Thank you for reading my book! I know you will be so inspired and motivated to step out into the greatness you have been given. Each one of us has a destiny and we need to fulfill this so we can live our lives with no regrets.

My name Derek actually means 'God's Destiny' in Hebrew, and I am very excited to write this book and to share my life's journey so far. This is not to show myself as some sort of hero, because I'm not, but to share things that have happened to me. This book is to encourage people and to show them that in life, anything can be possible. I feel blessed to be able to share this with you.

I'm here to write about my story as a blind person; a story of seemingly limitation and impossibility, and the process I lived through to do the impossible. I want to inspire millions of people to go past their limitations to what is possible for them and to take risks.

When something fills my heart, I want to accomplish it. I want to share the strategies I have used to step forward into my destiny and make dreams happen for myself, and for each person I meet. I am deeply driven to demonstrate that people can achieve whatever is in their heart, but they never can give up, they must forge through their fears.

I had a dream of surfing as a little boy and everyone told me it was impossible, that I could never learn. I refused to accept myself as limited. My life has been about how to overcome challenges and turn them into possibilities and progress. One of the first things I learnt is the art of overcoming obstacles. So, what if you allowed yourself to dream big? All of us have put limitations on our minds to achieve our goals. You can do what you had never given yourself permission to dream about. You can do it!

There is a story I want to tell you. There was a young Native American boy walking through his village. He came across his grandfather sitting on a rock, staring out into the forest. The young boy walked up to his grandfather and asked, "How are you today Grandfather?"

The grandfather answered, "Boy, I am at war within myself."

The boy asked, "Who is fighting?"

The grandfather said, "I have a grey wolf and a white wolf fighting to the death within me."

The boy asked, "Who will win?"

The grandfather said, "The one that I feed."

Your mind is exactly the same. Our thoughts are the food that feeds either our possibility or our fear. Whichever wolf you feed within yourself will become stronger and win the battle of your life. You cannot afford to feed the wrong wolf within you. Each thought and each word you speak over yourself, or to other people, either builds your courage and resolves to go beyond your limitations to the extraordinary, or binds you in the prison of your own self-constructed fears.

What if you committed to managing your mind and its focus so you made stronger the white wolf and starved off the grey wolf? What would your life be like? Who would you inspire? What lives could you change and how would you feel at the end of your life for having the courage to step outside your comfort zone and go for it? You only have one life that you've been given, so determine to be the 'you' that you are capable of being.

PROLOGUE

I remember when I had taken off on a wave in Hawaii. There I was, flying down the face of this enormous wave. I was yelling and so joyful, filled with happiness and gratefulness. It was a feeling of accomplishment and a feeling of power. I knew then that being blind was something small; it did not define me. I could manage my life around it and thrive. I realized that my happiness and purpose was more important to me than the possibility of dying in the ocean doing what I loved. My happiness was not about riding big waves; it was about doing something to teach people that they can also do extraordinary things in their life. They can push past their fears and do what everyone might have said is impossible to do, and do it anyway.

So why do I attempt the seemingly impossible? I am always searching for the perfect wave in the perfect place. I have a love affair with the ocean. All I can say is that I choose life, not death. I want to encourage you to get out there in your own life and pursue your goals, awaken deep-seeded hope in your hearts and help others to awaken to what is possible for them as well.

Derek Rabelo

CHAPTER 1.

MY DESTINY – AMAZING WHERE I AM NOW!

"**H**ELP I AM DROWNING!'"
"I don't want to die now. Has my life been so short on earth that this is it? There's so much more I want to do and achieve. Not now please," I was saying and also pleading to myself in a split second. The waves sounded like mountains and were crashing down upon me – like an avalanche wanting to devour all in its path. The waves were taking me unawares and pulling me under the huge wall of water. It was so terrifying and traumatic. I couldn't see anything and I couldn't breathe. I thought this was the end of me.

* * * *

This was one very important day in my short life as a surfer. It was a day that I nearly walked away from my destiny. I nearly threw away the wonderful opportunity that God had given me because I was afraid, yes, very afraid, and I'm not too proud to admit this. I didn't believe in the talent that was given to me and I honestly didn't understand it at that time.

I was surfing at a rather dangerous beach only after a month of my new 'adventure' and on reflection, I had to think again about this statement of 'adventure' when the start of my surfing career nearly came to an end.

A determined spirit

It was the evening of New Years Eve and I could sense that the weather was grey and cloudy. I can usually detect if the sun is shining or if it is dull and gloomy, or whatever the weather is doing. I was with a friend and he also confirmed to me about how dark it was becoming. This might seem strange but even though I was blind, my other senses always kick in powerfully. Probably not a great time to go out into the ocean! I was so oblivious to the surroundings, as I just wanted to surf at this 'famous' beach that I had heard so much about. I was so excited.

I was reliant on my friend and I could feel and experience the sounds and vibrations and the directions of the waves that were swelling up in the sea. And yes, they seemed to be increasing at a fast rate. Nevertheless, my enthusiasm was such that I didn't care too much at the time. Hey, I was surfing and that was so fantastic for someone who couldn't see the waves and what was coming towards me. That's all I wanted to do. My hyperactive personality, which I have always had, definitely kicked in and I wanted some adventure. Wasn't this what life was all about? Being blind was not a good start to life, but that is the way it was. So surfing was a huge challenge for me.

However, it wasn't until my father gave me a present of a surfboard on my seventeenth birthday that I, as an only child, tried riding my first waves. I was so excited and determined to make this my sport. This is what I had been longing to do for the last few years – this was my dream. Being blind was not going to stop me. No… not me. I wanted it all.

The area I was surfing in Brazil, where I lived, was quite remote and was next to the piers where the ships brought all the products into the area. An international mining company in Brazil was operating in that area. Container ships from all over the world were being unloaded and mud would fall into the ocean, making it very treacherous. The powder from the mines was blown all over the ocean, so the water was black too. Not a great place or environment to surf in!

As the trucks were being loaded and unloaded, there was a great deal of noise. The clamour from the boats and the machines made it very difficult for me. I couldn't hear the sound of the waves coming towards me, and this is very important when I'm out in the ocean. I rely on this. The reefs were also in my path and the dreaded sea creatures with their spikes were lazing around on the rocks, waiting for their latest victim, and there were always plenty of them. It is really a dangerous place to surf. Why was I at that place? Well, my dad always told me how good the waves were here, but always said very strongly that it was dangerous. It didn't matter though, I was determined to surf here!

This was the first time I was surfing outside of my home break, where it was always a comfortable place to ride the waves. It was familiar. This place, to get on the peak where the waves break, is 20 minutes out. It's totally unfamiliar.

This particular day, I went to surf with my friend. My father had also told me, "Wherever and whenever you surf with anyone else, let me know." But sometimes I forgot to tell him…

It was not a smart thing to forget to tell my father I was going to surf on that beach, especially because it was the beach he was most concerned about. Even though my home break where I learnt to surf is a heavy beach break, at least there are no rocks or reefs or weird animals trying to stab me while I surfed! Forgetting to tell my dad I was going to surf near the pier was a bad mistake! What was I thinking?

Up for the challenge

My good friend Magno, told me that surfing on the pier beach is something really challenging and hard for even advanced surfers. On the other hand, I always heard my dad say that I would get the best waves of my life surfing at that beach. It was perfect. (That was the part I listened to!) Not many people surf at that place because it is more than one kilometer from the shore.

So listening to my father and a few other people who have surfed in that place made me curious to experience that beach, even though I realized it would be something very dangerous. In my mind I said, *If I could get at least one wave that evening, my New Years Eve is going to be the best ever.* I was trying to imagine how good it would be to ride those waves. What a bad decision. Just thinking about how perfect that place could be and not the fact that I was putting my life at risk nearly cost me my surfing career! The trauma that this caused, almost gave me a reason to give up on surfing forever. In fact, I actually gave up surfing for a moment!

So how did I feel tackling this huge adventure? I have often pondered this. I guess I was really excited because it was the first time I was surfing somewhere different and that was important. I was also a bit scared because I knew it would not be easy and would be very challenging for me. I was not comfortable at all. But what was I to do? I think there was a mixture of emotions. Imagine: not only was I surfing somewhere unknown with only my friend beside me and it was an explosive ocean, but also I was blind! Was I crazy? Well, when you are a keen surfer, you will attempt anything, right?

When we first arrived there, the wind was blowing very strong; in fact, it was more like a gale. I was not very relaxed to start, and when we were paddling out, I felt the situation was not for me at all. I had a weird feeling. Then my friend caught a wave and I was there on my own. It was very frightening. All alone out there, in a wild and furious ocean and I could sense it was getting darker.

The waves were breaking on the reefs. At first, I didn't get any waves at all and I was paddling to the outside, far out into the ocean. Suddenly, a whole set of massive waves appeared and landed very heavily on me. They pushed me down and I got pounded. I was terrified. I paddled up a steep wall, up and up, and then the wave shut me down. It threw me down and broke on me. It was too late. I couldn't duck dive. I was trapped undewater. It was the most horrifying experience because I couldn't see anything – I didn't know where I was, what was happening to me or which way was up! . Other surfers were oblivious to me being held under. They didn't know I was blind so didn't think to help me. I couldn't blame them.

As I was under the water for a very long time, I started to panic. I couldn't even see what was going on. I ended up on the rocks where the sea creatures were waiting to spike me. *Where am I?* I was shouting in my head. More waves came and pushed me to the bottom of the ocean. This was now becoming quite terrifying because I couldn't breathe. I honestly didn't know what to do. How could I keep doing this? I couldn't get any air and I thought I was going to die. These were my thoughts as I struggled with the tumultuous churning of the waves as they conitnued to crash down on me. They showed no mercy.

I was thinking, *Why am I surfing? This doesn't bring joy. I am about to die. I'll stop doing this if I can just get out of this situation alive.*

Any surfer who has experienced this wonders if they will survive – let alone when you can't see – and I was not very experienced in the ocean. Fortunately, I remembered that I had a leg rope attached to my surfboard, so I used this to climb up and up and found my way to the surface. It was a miracle I could find my way to fresh air. I was so frightened. I was vomiting water and scared to breathe. I was calling out loud to my friend, trying to find him, but there was no response. He couldn't hear me, and then more waves got me and took me down again.

I hung onto my surfboard for dear life and the waves finally brought me to the shore. As you can imagine, I was extremely relieved to make it back to shore, and of course, to be alive. Wow, to be alive after that ordeal was a miracle. I can testify that miracles *do* happen.

Understandably, the experience left me completely shattered, to say the least. I was so scared and I didn't want to surf ever again. I told myself. that the cost was too great. I was blind. *There must be something else for me to do with my life that was not so dangerous*, I thought.

Never give up

On my way home I was thinking I would sell all my surf gear and my surfboard. However, the sad and distressing thing was that I didn't know what to do with my life. As I mentioned before, I thought when I was under the water that if I survived this, I would stop surfing. Surfing was my love, so what was I to do now? I was passionate about my sport. If I gave up surfing, I would give up something that would make me happy and satisfied. It was my contact with nature and the water. I told my family and friends that this was the end of my surfing career, which amounted to one month.

At that time, I didn't know surfing would become my career. To think I almost gave it up. It was something that was given to me from God. But being blind, I was trying to understand how this would work if I kept going. How would my life be today if I had given this up? For one, I would not have met my beautiful wife.

I realized that I would have to persevere. This was my destiny and I couldn't walk away from it – no matter how terrifying the sport appeared to be. Something inside of me made me press forward and push through beyond my fears.

The message I learnt from this was not to give up. I had to keep going, even in great difficulties. If I had let that accident take away my passion and the talent given to me, what would I do? Where would I be now? It could have changed my life completely. I could have gone into depression and after many years, regret that I had stopped.

This is how my surfing career began. Not a good start, but it made me think about what was in my heart; what actually motivated me and made me determined to change my thinking and continue on. It wasn't an easy decision and I had to turn around and think about the cost, which I hadn't really thought about before. When you are faced with some sort of trauma, it helps you to stop and think about what you really want in life; what you are called to do. What will ultimately satisfy you and what your future is meant to become.

But let me say that surfing rocks! I believe it is the best sport in the world. Even as a young person, I thought this way. It is wonderful having the wind and salt air blowing in my face. I feel alive when I'm in the water. I love the challenge of sensing the vibrations of the waves. Being blind it is imperative that I know what the waves are doing: such as if they are big or small, how far apart they are coming. I also need to understand what the weather is doing, which fortunately, I am able to do. My sensory perceptions are highly developed as they are in people who have a disability.

I am now surfing around the world as a professional surfer, but when I remember that surf, it still sends a shiver down my spine. I will never forget the fear of being held under those huge waves and thinking I was going to die. Even though the waves on that day were far smaller than the big waves I am now riding, I vowed never to surf in that area again and to this day, I haven't.

CHAPTER 2.

I CAME INTO THIS WORLD SCREAMING!

A nd kicking… not just crying like most babies. Oh no, not me, but *screaming*, according to my father.

Apparently my eyes were a bit closed and slanting and my hair was standing up on end. Wow, what a sight I must have been. This is the first glimpse my parents had of me. They were so overwhelmed. Who was this baby? I was very different to look at, but at that time of my birth, there was no indication there was anything wrong. My parents just loved me and thought I was the most beautiful baby in the world!

It very soon became apparent that things were not right with their little baby.

* * * *

A Tricky Relationship

Let me take you back to when my parents first met. My mother, Lia, and father, Ernesto, met at the local gym, where they both worked out. They knew their health and fitness was extremely important, so they embarked on a fitness program. They enjoyed their workout: my father flexing his muscles and my mother wanting to show off her exercise ability. And yes, they did notice each other, probably while working the treadmill and pumping some iron. Dad flirted with her at first, as he found her very appealing to the eye, which was wonderful for my mother. She wanted him to notice her; she was definitely attracted to him.

At first, they formed a great friendship then they began to date. As it happened, my mother developed a strong love for my father. "I really loved him and wanted to marry him," she explained.

My father regrettably did not feel as strongly for my mother at the time. In fact, he told her that the relationship was very hard. This naturally was not what my mother wanted to hear. "Perhaps I didn't love her enough, so we ended the relationship," my father said. My mother was very hurt and upset over this, as she had fallen in love with him. She didn't want to meet anyone else. To her, he was 'the one.' Young love doesn't always run smooth.

A Little Surprise
However, as things transpired, the relationship took another momentous turn. "I discovered that I was pregnant at the age of 24 years," my mother said, remembering those sad and difficult times. "I was devastated and didn't know what to do. I was just so terrified. I was really scared when I first realized what had happened. I mean, it was not acceptable then for an unmarried girl to be pregnant. But what was I to do?"

This was the difficult situation my mother was confronted with. She finally found the courage to tell my father. He of course, panicked. "What should we do?" he asked fearfully. "I don't want to get married" He was faced with some tough decisions to make.

They were both confronted with a huge dilemma. This was not

accepted in our society at that time and they faced with possibly being ostracized. Yes, this was a likely scenario and they were both extremely worried. There were, of course, some alternatives, but...

"Then Lia told me she was going to the doctor to have the pregnancy terminated," my father said, thinking back to those very challenging times. However, my mother was extremely scared and both of them had a very bad feeling about going through with the termination. They just didn't feel it was the right thing to do, but what were they going to do about this? My mother had at first said she wanted to have an abortion, but when it came to going through with this, in her heart she didn't really want to go ahead with this procedure. It was really against what she believed in. "Then I agreed with her and so we went to see the doctor," my father explained. "During a conversation with the doctor I felt something touching me. It was a strange sensation. Maybe it was a sign? I can't really explain it. Then when we left I told Lia, 'Let's not do it – I'll take my responsibility as a father and I'll look after the child, but I don't want to get married.' So we didn't go ahead with the abortion, which I am eternally grateful for. We wouldn't have had this beautiful and wonderful son, of whom I am so proud."

Breaking the news
"My pregnancy was not very easy," my mother said with some sadness. "I was trying to hide my pregnancy from my mother for four months because Ernesto and I weren't brave enough to tell her. We knew that she wouldn't accept it because we were not married. I was struggling to break the news to her."

After much deliberation, my father and mother finally confided in my paternal grandmother, Cleuza, trying to be positive and saying I would be the first grandchild. That should have been a little light shining through the darkness – something optimistic to think about. They naturally thought she would understand and be excited at the thought of a new baby coming into the family. Well, this is what they hoped for because they knew my maternal grandmother Laura would not be happy about the news – with no marriage proposal. In fact there was no sign of any marriage on the horizon.

My mother continued. "I was so scared to tell my mother, Laura. I really didn't know how she would react, although I knew she would be very angry with me because my mother was very strict. She eventually found out when I was four months' pregnant. I didn't tell her; it was Ernesto's mum, Cleuza, who told her. When she found out, she wasn't happy at all. This was the lowest period in my life. First of all Ernesto didn't love me and wouldn't marry me, then I was having a baby out of wedlock. It definitely wasn't easy for me."

My mother wanted to go to her brother's house to escape the situation at home to avoid all the embarrassment and ridicule that she would have to face, but she didn't go because my grandmother helped her to get a job making curtains and provided an apartment for her to live in. She was kept busy and that would have been a good thing.

Things still didn't go well for my mother while she was pregnant. "When I was 24 weeks, I started to bleed very heavily and the doctors recommended that I rest in bed," she stated. "So Ernesto and his brothers carried me up to my mother-in-law's house so she could take care of me. For three days I couldn't stand up. *What else can go wrong?* I thought to myself. *Haven't I been through enough?* These thoughts were going through my head over and over again."

25th May 1992

My mother finally went into labour and was rushed to the hospital. I made my entrance into the world at 5 a.m. on that day.

"The birth went smoothly, thank God," my father shared. "I decided to give the name Derek to my son, after the Hawaiian surfer Derek Ho, as it was my dream for him to become a great surfer, as I am a surfer myself. I loved the sport and was determined my child would follow me. Well, I hoped so anyway. Lia fortunately agreed with the name I had wanted.

There were a lot of expectations from my father's side, as I would be their first grandchild. Even though my mother and father were not married, everyone was excited to have a new baby in the family. So that at least helped to ease any tension that would have existed. The whole situation was very stressful, though. My mother found the whole situation difficult to deal with, as she really loved my father. She wanted her child to be part of a traditional family unit, but my father wouldn't alter his decision and she was devastated.

Reality sets in

My mother's apartment was right below where my father lived, so everything was in good order and being prepared for me to come home. Unfortunately, my mother was not happy, especially when my father went out at night to parties by himself and would come home in the early hours of the morning. This is not what she wanted for her life. She wanted a normal, loving family life, where her child could grow up with a mother *and* father. She was scared, as she didn't know what lay ahead for her.

"I would usually hear her crying, so I would always go there to visit her," my father said. "After a while I would end up living in her apartment with her. So we were back together, trying to make this work. It felt like we were going well, but I knew this wouldn't end up good because there was no love from my side towards her." So here was my mother: an unmarried woman, pregnant and her boyfriend who didn't love her. It was a very difficult and unhappy time for her.

"When we arrived home and it was time for Derek's first shower, I wanted to give that privilege to Lia's mom, as she had looked after her own seven children and 20 grandchildren." My father also invited a friend of his to film this special occasion, as he was the only person he knew with a camera. (it wasn't easy to find a camera in those days.) There was a lot of joy during the shower, according to my father. It was a very special family occasion.

Something was not right
My father had noticed something was wrong on the sixth day and my mother also knew something was not right, but then my parents and the doctors discovered that I could not see. Straight away, my mother and father were in total shock and disbelief. They couldn't believe it – surely there was a misunderstanding, a misdiagnosis. How could this happen? What could they do? The drama permeated my whole extended family. As if the circumstances in which I was conceived wasn't bad enough, now this.

"When Derek first opened his eyes, they were totally blue, which I found weird because Lia and I didn't have blue eyes," his father remembered. "This apparently is the first sign that a baby has glaucoma." However, this was only my father's assumption, so there was a great deal of panic at this time. My parents didn't know what to think, so they took me to a doctor to ask him to explain what was wrong with my eyes. The doctor told them they should take me to an ophthalmologist immediately. Then more panic settled in.

"My first reaction was one of the worst reactions I have ever had," my mom stated, with a great deal of hurt in her heart. "It was a terrible feeling that a mother could have when you find out your child is blind. Honestly I didn't believe the dreadful news. Inside, I couldn't believe what was going on."

Having to come to grips with this devastating news, my parents immediately took me to the best doctor they could find who recommended they see a paediatrician immediately. My parents found this extremely difficult to deal with. They were devastated.

My father exclaimed, "Yes, I definitely knew things were not good. I felt so helpless. What could I do? How could I help my son? Surely this was not happening to us." It was a time of utter despair, a feeling of helplessness for my parents, and in fact all of my family members.

Difficult journey ahead

My parents made the decision to do everything they could to help me. They wanted the very best for their child. My father's mother, Cleuza, went with them to see the doctor, as my mother had just given birth and needed some support.

My father went on to explain, "When we arrived there, the doctor just looked at Derek's eyes and said, 'Hey dad, mom and grandma, I'm so sorry to tell you this, but your baby has severe congenital glaucoma. I cannot do anything here, but he needs surgery as soon as possible. There is a hospital 600km from here in another state, which is world-renowned in glaucoma surgery. I would recommend you take him there.'"

My parents at this stage thought this could be turned around with the right surgery. My father continued, "All of us were crying and we went back home. I was thinking and wondering, 'How will Derek's life be? How will his future be? Who is going to look after him, when we're not here anymore?' All these questions were going around in my head."

The next morning, my father called that particular hospital the doctor had recommended to try to get an appointment urgently, as they knew time was of the essence. My parents had to move as quickly as possible, as they were so stressed about my problem and wanted it fixed right away. I was their number one priority. The hospital was a private one and quite expensive. My father had a good job at that time, so they could afford the surgery at that hospital. They drove ten hours inland to where the hospital was based.

My mother had an uncle who lived in that same city as the hospital, so my mother and father could stay in his house. He was very happy to receive us, as he knew my father would go fishing with him. They had grown up together in their hometown. However, he didn't know of my plight concerning my eyes at that time. It was a blessing that we could stay there."

My parents then took me to see the doctor and he informed them it was essential that I undergo eye surgery as soon as possible. He did explain to them that it would be a very difficult operation. The eye pressure was very high. The normal eye pressure is 11, but my eye pressure was 27, which was way too high. That was the reason for the blue colour of my eyes. The high pressure in the eyes also burns the cornea.

As the surgery was urgent I was booked in for the operation the next day at 7 a.m. However, there were even more problems. "Derek was used to drinking breast milk every hour," my father said. "He was never without milk for over two hours, but because of the surgery the next day, he had to fast for 12 hours. He really suffered so much. When it was 9 p.m. the night before, he was already screaming all the time because he was so hungry. We had so much compassion that he had to go through all this pain because he could not have any milk. No one could sleep because he was crying for the whole night."

In the morning, the surgery was delayed by three hours. Of course, I don't remember any of this, , but I can only imagine what babies and small children must go through when faced with this dilemma of not being able to eat before an operation. In reality, parents must also suffer as they hear their little ones crying.

"Once the surgery finished, the doctor called me to talk about it," my father remembers. "He said that the surgery was really hard and also that Derek's eyeball wasn't a normal shape. There was more drama when the doctor called us after the surgery to see Derek, and when we saw him, well, there was blood around his eye and on his blanket, then we started to cry so much to see him in that situation. He was only 28 days old. It was a terrible time."

"I think then I realized it was actually true that he had no sight when the first surgery took place," Lia said. "I then knew this is real; I have to go through that, and Derek was only a tiny baby."

Straight after the surgery, my eye pressure was apparently back to 28 again, so my parents were incredibly disappointed. They were hoping that the operation would be successful and everything would be 'normal'. The doctor told my parents to not give up, that they could operate again in a while, but it was totally up to my parents, whatever they decided to do. This was a huge dilemma for them; whether to put me through this ordeal again.

Holding onto hope
All the operations took place in Belo Horizonte Citi. My parents came back each time very sad, but still with hope. They were not going to give up – hope was the substance that they hung on to. Hope kept them going and kept them strong. What do we do without hope?

"I was the only one in my family who wasn't a Christian, and with Lia it was the same," my father added. "But she started to slowly walk with Jesus a few months before Derek was born. We always had the support of our parents and brothers and their church was praying constantly for us and especially for Derek."

It was wonderful to have so many people praying for me. The travel back home for us was really hard. It is about 10 hours driving, going through mountains and there are many difficult turns, as the roads were very rough.

My parents were disappointed. When they arrived back home, they had to explain to family, friends and everyone who was nearby about my situation - that I was blind and the surgery was not successful. That would have been extremely frustrating and very sad to share this with others. They were hoping that good news would prevail, but this was not the case. My parents consequently made a second appointment for more surgery. They wanted to try everything they could to have my sight restored.

"'My Little chick', which was his nickname, was starting to smile at us and was developing his movements," my father said. "Always when he was laying down, he used to move his arms in front of his eyes. This was really sad to see because we were sure he was realizing that he couldn't see perfectly. He knew that there was something going on, that something was not right, even at his young age. Maybe he was only seeing some shapes. I don't know."

Again, my parents prepared to make the long trip to Belo Horizonte Citi, which was a very intense time and they were terrified. They stayed in the same house with my mother's uncle. The preparation for the second surgery was very mild. However, the same difficulties were experienced as before for the first surgery, which was very distressing again. There was once again another 12 hours of fasting and another delay for the surgery. I was crying much more this time and the neighbours were so distraught that they asked my parents what was happening.

After this second operation, the doctor once again called my parents to speak to them. Unfortunately the eye pressure was high again. My parents were very upset and thought it was not worth putting me through any more operations. It was too traumatic. However, the doctor encouraged them not to give up, to try surgery one more time, so it was a very difficult decision for them to make. All of the treatment was private, encompassing international techniques and included doctors with all the best knowledge. The hospital was the best in Brazil and one of the best eye hospitals in the world, so all this helped my parents to then decide to at least consult with the doctors.

On the following day, they had an appointment with Dr Felicio, who is a world expert in glaucoma. He is the specialist who performed all the surgeries. At that appointment, he said to my parents that the situation remained the same, that it didn't make sense to use any eye drops to make the eyeball high-pressure to go lower. It would not work.

The doctor said there was something new that they were working on and it was quite successful. It was a valve made from silicon that would be implanted inside the eyeball. It would require them inserting a silicon valve. He suggested it might be worth a try because they had experienced some good results with people who had tried it. But it was up to my parents to decide if they wanted to go down this path. However, the valve came from overseas and it was very expensive, so therein lay the dilemma for my family.

"The company that I was working for covered my family and me with health insurance, but I still had to pay a part of it," my father went on to say. "For the remaining amount that I had to pay, my company gave me a credit so I could be paid monthly, as the amount was really high.

I would do anything to give sight to my son. Anything. I would do the possible and also the impossible so he could see."

Miracles do happen don't they? When this third surgery took place, my parents were still paying off the first and second surgeries, so there was a huge strain on them financially. This added to the pressure that was descending upon them in all directions, emotionally, mentally and financially. This was their life at the time and they knew they had to fight their way through this.

I was one year of age at the time of my third surgery. My parents gave me a lot of love, care and support, but they were really suffering. I don't know how they were able to cope, although it was less stressful in that I now didn't need to be fed all the time. So at least I could cope with waiting for the operation and not eating any food.

My father said, "One day after the surgery, right before our appointment with the doctor, something really shook me. I saw my boy playing around, jumping, running, singing and talking by himself. I realized that even though he was blind and just had surgery and had plaster on his eyes, he was a happy boy. That was when I woke up and realized and I told myself that my child is actually very happy."

Unfortunately, even after the expense of inserting the valve, the third surgery was not successful. I can only think about how they would have felt after all of this. Three surgeries and no success. My parents broke down; their beautiful baby boy could not see the wonderful world that surrounded him. The exquisiteness of God's creation was hidden, like a dark veil was over my eyes, and it seemed like over my very being.

"Every time Derek went to surgery, I thought in my heart that Derek would come out being able to see," Lia said. "But that was not the truth; that was not happening. I was trying to will him to see. When, after each surgery, he still was unable to see, I always thought he was going to regain his sight and that kept me strong over the years. I have never really accepted Derek was blind, but that doesn't mean that I was angry. I always had lots of faith. Faith kept me going a lot. I never was angry at God and never questioned God and asked why."

When I stop and consider what my parents and the rest of my family went through, I stand in awe of their commitment and love towards me. I don't think I could have achieved as much if not for their support. My father couldn't give any more information about my birth and operation, as he was crying so much. Remembering this time brought back so many disturbing memories and so much heartache.

CHAPTER 3.

LOVE CONQUERS ALL

The one thing that remains with me as a young child and throughout my life is that love conquers all. All I know is that without the total and unconditional love of my parents and my extended family, I would not have survived as well as I did. I would not have had the wonderful life that I have experienced. Thank you so much to my family and friends.

"When Derek was already nine months old, he had the habit of going to sleep at around 8:00 p.m. and waking up at 5:00 a.m. in the morning. He would play alone in the crib for a while. He was contented to do this. He was already standing, holding the grid of the crib. It was in the corner of the room, a few feet from our bed.

"One day, I woke up with him crying, as he usually did every morning. But this time something struck me, and to this day, it will not leave my memory. He was standing crying and facing the wall and not toward our bed. This was such a very sad thing to see. I cried at seeing him, not realizing where we were. It broke my heart. I remember this scene constantly. My thoughts for the future of my blind son were ... well, very hard to think about. I felt so upset and distraught. But on the positive side, my love just soared for my little boy. I thought to myself, 'My beautiful little boy will have a wonderful life. He will do something great and I will always make sure he knows how loved he is'. That incident created something in me, something in my heart, that changed my perspective in the life my beautiful son would have."

My mother explained her emotions in coping with me as a small child. "After the surgeries, when we brought Derek home, I prayed a lot and kept strong in my faith. It was not always so easy and I cried a lot, but that was my base for coping. I was learning something new each day. I was asking God to keep me strong and how to look after my child. I had to learn to look after a blind child, but I learnt this so wonderfully well because I believed God would give me great capacity to raise my son, and I have never waivered from this. God gave me Derek because he knew I was able to manage him."

Eventually, my parents were becoming a bit more optimistic about my future and coming to terms with the fact that I may not ever see. It was difficult for them, but they wanted the very best for me. However, there were many hurdles to overcome. There were times of despair and sadness, but also times of hope. Hope in that I could lead a normal life, as much as possible, and that faith would see me through. Well, others who were blind had led good and productive lives, so it was considered that I could. Why not? I was so blessed that my family members were so positive.

"When Derek was a bit over one year old, he was getting used to not being able to see," my father said. "However, since the first surgery when he was in the hospital, I decided I definitely didn't want to have another child. It was a big decision to make, but I knew it was the right one for me, even though the midwife who delivered Derek told us that probably his glaucoma was not genetic. However, she explained if we decided that we would have another child one day, it would be good to have pre-pregnancy counseling.

"The doctor who performed the operation also told us that what Derek had was only something that happened to him personally. Nevertheless, I still didn't want to take the risk. This had been all too traumatic for me, Lia and of course, Derek. I knew this was right at the time, but it was not an easy conclusion to come to, particularly as the years progressed."

A typical boy
Apparently, as I was starting to grow taller, so was my energy level, which was really a good thing. I am not sure if my parents thought the same. I was awake most of the time and I tired out anyone who was looking after me. No one could keep up with me. The positive side was that I was healthy, apart from some allergies I had. I was always into everything, according to my father. Not wrong things, but typical toddler amusements and games and getting into all sorts of trouble. Everyone was tired and worn out except me! I just wanted to keep moving and experience all that life had to offer me. The wonderful side to all of this is that I was very happy and loved by everyone. The love I was surrounded by kept me going and enabled me to lead a normal life. Well, as much as possible…

I don't know how my life would have turned out if I hadn't experienced this, but I must have kept the household hopping! I believe there were many dramas with my over-exuberant personality. I wanted to experience everything and even though I couldn't see, I compensated in other areas. I could feel, I could sense things, I had acute hearing. I learnt to develop in those areas. I had to.

My mother was always very protective of me. "I had lots of safety precautions in place for Derek and I was always worried that he would get hurt," she explained. "Most of the time I would be on hand looking after him so he would not get hurt because he was too hyperactive. I couldn't always keep up with him; I was really exhausted. It was not easy in terms of taking care of him. It is different from a father's role. I don't mean his dad was not looking after him, but as a mom, you want to protect your child more and have him under your wings. The father is more... like a father.

"Derek always wanted to play and to do anything that he was not allowed to do and anything that was dangerous – like climb a tree, or jump out of the window, or ride a bicycle. He would do anything that was hazardous and was not really allowed for a blind child. I always wanted to keep him safe and I was always on the run. For instance, when he was running around, I was trying to protect him because someone might try to fight him, so I had to watch him constantly. My time was all for him. Maybe sometimes he would run and bump someone because he couldn't see and that person might get mad because they wouldn't know he was blind – until they saw this in his eyes. It was constant, to say the least."

Father and son
My father added: "In my job, I worked for ten years, where I had a shift where I would work six days at night and have two days off. This was convenient, as I would have a lot of hours to spend with Derek. That helped me build a really great friendship and partnership between my son and me. We were going to the beach every day and riding bicycles. This was a wonderful bond that we developed and I treasure it to this day. There is nothing greater than to connect closely with your children."

There was one instance my father told me about in my early years which was quite hilarious and this explains my love of adventure. I was about 18 months old and there was a huge storm and it was raining quite heavily. My father called me and said, "Let's play." That was like music to my ears. "Derek made this cute face at my suggestion like, *oh really, let's do it*. It's the same face he still makes today," my father said with a big smile. We went onto the street and the rain was coming down like buckets were being emptied from the heavens. When my mother saw us out in the rain she screamed at dad, "Are you crazy? He's going to get sick. Don't do it."

My father and I didn't listen to her, of course. We were having such a great time. It was wonderful and we were so happy. My mother called her parents to tell them we were playing in the rain and it was wrong, as I would get sick. Everyone was frightened for me. But she didn't understand the importance of the bond and friendship that we were developing. Although I do understand her concern, most mothers would probably react in this way. She was only thinking of what was best for me.

"After that he always wanted to go and play whenever there was rain," my dad said. "This was a joke between us, but it was a wonderful joke and one that cemented our father and son relationship."

A love for water
When I was about two years old, I had a tricycle and I loved the fast action and would run over everyone and everything. We lived on a small farm and I drove everywhere that I could, but my favorite place was playing in the river. Dad would put 'floaties' on me to make sure I kept above water. When I was two years old, I was already able to float, even without my floaties. My father said, "That's because I would always throw him from the river bank into the water. Then I would run and jump quickly so I could catch Derek. But, as a typical toddler, he always wanted more. He had so much energy and I found it difficult sometimes

to keep up with him. He just never ever tired, but I certainly did! How does a parent keep up with this?

"He also loved it when we would go swimming. I would put him on my back. He would hold onto my shoulders and I would dive with him under the water. It was a challenge to keep up with him and his boundless energy. I admit I had to be careful all the time to avoid any dramas that could have occurred in the water because Derek didn't know any fear, and this was particularly significant when he was in the water. He just loved it. Yes, nothing has changed. However, I did arrange swimming lessons for him to be on the safe side."

At the age of two, my parents bought me my first boogie board and I still have that in my house today. It is so very special to me. I had so much fun on that board and my father would pull me around with a leash on the river and on the beach. I loved being on the beach and my father would take me out when the waves were a bit bigger and dive under to give me some excitement and, oh, how I enjoyed it. I felt like I was in heaven. I remember laughing a lot when the waves would break on me. I guess my love for the ocean started from a very early age. It seemed as though my future was being sealed. The waves captivated me, even though I couldn't actually see them, but I could sense the vibrations in the water and feel the movement. This was very challenging and exciting for me. I didn't want it to end.

My father bought an old motorcycle, but petrol was very expensive, so we used this just to go around the small farm we lived on and on small trips. I really loved riding on it. Dad often took me with him and I would be sitting on the front, hugging the tank really hard. That was a great bonding time. It always made me happy and it was so exciting; a great adventure to a small boy. I loved the adventure of whirling around on this motorcycle. The faster it went, the better.

I had many wonderful bonding times with my father, playing in the mud in the rain, on the tricycle, the boogie board and the motor cycle. I felt so blessed. My father allowed me to touch the bike and rub my hands all over it to feel how heavy it was. It was another exciting thing to experience. The motor bike was on a stand and my father showed me the exhaust pipe and told me how hot it was and dangerous and that I should never play around with it. But, I was a young boy…

My first accident

My father explained, "After a few months, I arrived home and I saw Derek running from the gate towards the house and then come back to the gate again, crying. I went to see what was happening with Derek and there was blood all over him. It was everywhere and I couldn't stop the bleeding. I had no idea what had happened. I put him under the shower because I couldn't find where he hurt himself at first. Of course, I was extremely concerned. I happened to see his hand and his little finger – the nail was gone and the top of the finger was also gone, along with the nail.

"I still didn't know what happened. When he was calm, I asked him to show me where he hurt himself. In the backyard there was a plastic covering that my brother had left there and Derek told me he was climbing up and fooling around, as he always loved playing around like a monkey. He actually looked like a monkey when he was climbing! I told him not to play around there anymore; it was dangerous."

After many months, my conscience must have got the better of me, as I hadn't told my father the truth and I was feeling quite bad. I knew it wasn't right. I called out to him and said, "If I was to tell you something, do you promise not to give me a slap?" I was trying to protect myself as I summoned up the courage to say what really happened. He would often give me a slap, as I was always doing silly things. My father tried to keep me on track, keep me under control to stop me from doing what could be potentially dangerous for me. He assured me he would not give me a slap. I had to own up and tell the truth. I don't know why it occurred to me at that time to say this, but I just had to do it. Then I told him that it was not on the plastic roof that I hurt my finger that day. I took him by the hand to show him. I took him towards the motorcycle and said, "It was just here, Daddy."

My father used to leave the motorcycle always on the center stand, so I showed him what I did. I had spun the wheel and I put my finger in the middle of the chain while it was spinning - that's what really happened. I must admit remembering that I felt better once I had told my father the truth. "Derek was telling me this event with the cutest face ever," my father said. "Even though he deserved a little slap because he lied to me, I found it a bit funny, so I didn't punish him and I had given my word."

My uncle Evandro and his wife had a son called Lucas. We grew up together, having lots of fun on the small farm we were both living on. My father said, with a little smirk on his face, "Derek would always do things that would often blow our minds. He was very adventurous and loved to keep us all 'on our toes'. Oh, I'm not sure how I kept up with him. For a blind little boy, he sure was full of life. Once I heard my father say, 'That boy will be different." I didn't give a great deal of credit to what my Dad was saying at the time. 'This boy will be extremely different,' he would say a number of times. I was not even three years old when he told me that, which turned out to be very prophetic.

"Derek never complained about being blind and he never questioned anything – well not that I remember him doing this," my mother said. "He was always happy and always very playful – always until today."

When I was more independent, I started to walk along the beach more and I was hearing the waves crashing around me and smelling the salt air. It was so invigorating and I felt as though I was being drawn to the ocean and becoming more interested in the surf. I absolutely loved this; it was like it was in my blood. As I mentioned before, I received a boogie board from my father and this inspired me even more. Since then I loved the water. The first time I got a surfboard, I was a kid and I wanted to stand up on the board. I felt alive.

When I was about three or four years old, there was a surf shop, which belonged to a friend of my father and uncle's on the side of my mother's. I used to go there and play around, touching all of the surfboards and asking about the surf. I loved doing that. I would escape from my mother's shop that was only one minute away and walk to the surf-shop. I loved to touch the surfboards and this made the owner of the store quite nervous because sometimes I would cause a break in the boards. I would bump them accidentally and he was not happy. I suppose looking back, he wished I wasn't there, but I was enthralled with them and I just loved touching and feeling the boards.

My childhood was very happy, even though I was blind, but I learnt to accept this and because I was so loved at home and had a wonderful family life, it helped me enormously with my disability. However, I don't want to call it a disability because I always felt so loved and also believed I could still do anything I wanted to. There was a strong belief system operating in me and this is a wonderful thing to have. It is vital to achieving and reaching your destiny in life. I wouldn't be where I am now without it.

CHAPTER 4.

SCHOOL – OH HAPPY DAYS!

Finally, at the ripe old age of three years old, I started preschool. My father, however, was a bit reluctant to send me. He said, "I didn't want to put him into preschool yet. I wanted to enjoy more time with my 'adventurous' partner. Honestly, I was trying to avoid a situation that I already knew we would have to go through."

When I was finally old enough, my father took me to the school to sign me up. The classes start at the beginning of February in Brazil and I would be turning four in May 1996. I was taken to the best and nicest private school in my hometown and it was quite a traditional school. My father explains, "I asked if I could have a chat with the principal of the school, who was also the owner. I explained to her my son's situation: that he was blind. Straight away, she indicated to me she didn't want to accept me at her school, and this was quite distressing. 'Why would she be dismissive of my son?' I asked myself. I left the school really upset, but already I was thinking that we had to march forward. I had to think this way. I could sense we would have lots of problems and hard times. But what could we do?

"Then I went to another small private preschool. At this school, the principal was also the owner. When I told her the situation of my son, her first reaction was one of kindness and showing me she really wanted to help us. She took me around to show me the school and introduced me to the teachers and also the teacher who would be looking after Derek. We were, and still are, very grateful to everyone at the school: from the receptionist, cleaners, teachers, security and the leaders and all the staff of that school. All of them gave Derek a great deal of kindness, help and love during the two years he was there. Our family will never forget this."

On the first day, my father brought me to my class. Normally when you drop children to the school, particularly for the first time, they cry when the parents leave and they don't want to stay alone. So my father and mother were extremely worried about me. But nope – not me, I didn't cry. No one needed to worry about me. I was cool.

My parents had a good talk to me and explained everything that would take place and I was very excited about starting school. My father explained this would be the school I would attend every day and I would be without mommy and daddy. I would have to make new friends and be obedient to the teachers. "When I said that, Derek ran into the school and started to get involved with all the kids and then play," my father remembered. "I stayed there for 20 minutes and he didn't care about leaving me. I went to tell him that I was going home and he had to stay and he said, 'Okay Daddy, I already know it.' Well, so much for worrying about my son and how he would cope without us. I felt a bit redundant, but on the other hand it was a relief knowing we didn't have to worry about him starting school.

"Funny thing was when I came to pick Derek up at the end of the day, I said, 'Let's go home Derek and have lunch and we'll come back tomorrow.'

He said, 'No way Daddy, I want to play ball.' I said, 'No, everyone is going home.' Then I said again, 'No everyone is going home the class has finished, we come back tomorrow.' Then Derek started to cry and he was saying that I was lying to him because he was blind and he thought all the kids were already there. Then I explained, 'Tomorrow you'll meet them again.'"

So, as you can see, I didn't have a problem with starting school. I loved it. I stayed there for two years and then my preschool days came to an end. It was time for the 'big stuff' - primary school.

Primary school
So the big day had just arrived to go to primary school. At that time, there was a huge advertisement from the government on the television about the importance of kids with disabilities to be studying in regular schools. It was to be like a social inclusion. They also believed the students would have a better performance level than in a special school for the disabled. My father already had planned to sign me up in a regular school before seeing the advertisement. He wanted me to be integrated into a normal school. However, my dad knew that serious problems could arise that would make us very upset - and he was right.

My father said, "Derek has a really good memory and I thought with a voice memory device and Braille writer machine, he would go well at school. That advertising campaign made me really excited. But it was not easy. I had a lot of frustrating times. At that time I was able to pay for him to study in a nice school, a good quality school."

Unwanted
Once again, my father took me to the most traditional and the best and coolest school in my hometown. He wanted the very best for me and for that I am eternally grateful. "I was there talking with the principal

of this school, who was also the owner of the school," my father said. "I was there trying to sign up my son, explaining to the principal about his disability and she straight away said, 'We don't want your kid here.'

"I was mortified. I couldn't believe the way she confronted me and treated us. She put a lot of difficulties and excuses together for not having him. So I left the school heartbroken and disappointed. So my dream to see my son studying at this school was impossible; it was out of reality. It was the school I really wanted him to attend."

My father and I went to another excellent school and it was the same: they didn't want to accept me. What were we to do? My father was becoming increasingly anxious over the situation of my education, but he wasn't about to give up.

"Then I went to the last one: the third school and the last school in the city," my father revealed. "I went to have a chat with the principal and owner of the school. Talking with the principal was no different from the other principals. I explained to her about my son, but it was even worse. She didn't want my son there under any circumstances. The first two were not too bad, but this one was not very nice at all. She was very disrespectful with me and required me to hire a private teacher to be with him in the class.

"But I would have to pay for this if Derek went to that school and the teacher would have to be with him the whole time. These were the conditions she set down. It was just so disrespectful; it drove me crazy. I was out of my mind. Also, they were very mean. Then I thought about the advertisement, but in reality, it was bad. The regular schools would not accept a disabled child. It was a dreadful and untruthful advertisement. Then I asked myself, 'What now?'"

Unfortunately there were only those three excellent private schools in our city. The public schools in Brazil are really bad. He didn't want to put me in a special school, as it would not have been good for me. My father explained, "I knew Derek's potential and I knew it would drag him back in his development. I was thinking that my son needs to study, but if he's not in a private school, things would be very difficult and hard for him. It would be so hard for him because the public schools were not good."

A glimmer of hope

But thanks to God, the last hope showed up. There was a new school about to be launched in the city; a new private school. There was a family that had a building company and they were opening this school. A few years ago, they opened a university and now they were opening the school, which had classes from primary through to high school.

"When I arrived there, I felt at home," my father said. "The people responsible were the leaders and the principal of the school and members of the family who were the owners. There were two ladies. They were sisters and they were responsible for the school. So I felt really at home because those two ladies had dated my two brothers! It felt very comfortable. Talking with them, they showed they would help in every detail I needed help with. They also explained to me the level of how good this school was. So Derek was accepted and started to study there. I was so relieved and thankful to God for His provision."

When I started at this school, there were some class colleagues from preschool. I built a great friendship with everyone: the students, parents teachers, leaders, cleaning people, the food people and also the security guards of the school. Some of them I was already friendly with because they also worked in the same shopping complex where my father had a store. Everyone treated me with great love. My family and I were, and still are, very, very grateful to everyone in that school who received me. I remained at this school for my whole education until I graduated at 17 years of age.

I had a bit of a hard time, but nothing too bad. The books had to be made into Braille for me and they always took a long time to arrive. Not because of the school, but it was the supplier's and seller's fault. It caused some problems with my studies, as I was always trying to catch up and this put some stress on me. It was difficult enough being blind, let alone trying to draw level to my classmates.

A very busy kid

As I mentioned before, I was really hyperactive and also I was often bored in the classroom. Nothing really stimulated me. (I guess I'm not the only student who can honestly say this!) I soon began to do the craziest things. I was always playing around, doing stupid things. You could say I was a bit of a problem.

"I was thinking about my emotions when the time came for Derek to leave us and go to school," my father said. "At the beginning, I wondered if he would make it because of his blindness and because he was a real kid, very hyperactive and quite silly. But I must say, he was very smart. Once he reached primary school, he started to show his smartness and also his pranks. But all of us as his family were having a break from his pranks and his hyperactivity at least five hours a day because he was at school, so that was a positive. This was especially true for his mother. She had lost so much weight because she had to look after him a lot. That's how active he was; he was never still for a moment, always into everything. However, there were a few joyful moments in school time: the school games and parties for the kids. Derek would be entertained with anything. He was certainly such a character.

"In the first few years, we had a really hard time disciplining Derek.

Not actually with his studies, but in his behavior. Then the first sad thing happened. The psychologist of the school called me up and then she said, 'Father, we have lots of problems with Derek. He never stops and he never calms down and never lets the other students pay attention in class. He is really hyperactive, messing around a lot.' Then I thought, 'Are you saying do I need to remove him out of the school?' But then the psychologist said, 'I need you to take him to have some serious psychological treatments.'

"I agreed he was out of control and not normal and I would take him to start this treatment and I would let the psychologist know what happened. So I made the appointment and she did a lot of examinations. Then the report came back saying Derek was really hyperactive. One of the reasons for this was because of his blindness and this made his hyperactivity even worse. But that was what I was expecting. I knew that. It was not new to me."

I had to then go to a doctor and he wrote on two separate pieces of paper prescribing lots of medications. Then my family started to read about the medications on the paper and they were really strong. My parents never really liked this because these drugs could make everything worse, rather than help me. They knew medications could kill more than heal and as I was growing and getting older, they knew I could get better. Fortunately, they didn't give me any drugs. "I just talked to Derek a lot and his mom and grandma just prayed for him," my father exclaimed.

"At the school, I told Derek to say he was taking the medication the doctor prescribed. Not wanting to lie, but... They also asked me several times how the treatment was going and I said, 'Yes he's doing it.' They said they realized Derek was doing the treatment and that the psychologist was very good! Then they revealed he was getting better. But I thought it is really good saying prayers and giving some little slaps along the way. Prayer works wonders and miracles."

The judge and his daughter

One day, something quite bad happened. The school called my father saying there was an emergency and that he had to go to the school to pick me up as quickly as possible. "They told me not to worry because nothing really bad happened with Derek, but they would explain the situation to me when I arrived. Then I drove there like crazy wondering what this was all about. I honestly thought he was badly hurt, although the school assured me he was okay, so this gave me some relief. It was a long drive to the school. I knew he was hyperactive and sometimes two or three people looking after him was not enough.

"Apparently, Derek, with all his craziness, was running and bumped into a girl who was standing up on a chair. Then the girl fell off the chair with her legs opened and the chair hurt her private parts really badly and she was bleeding. The father of that girl was a judge and he came racing in a very furious and angry mood to the school to catch Derek. Regrettably, in Brazil, the authorities think they can do everything and abuse their authority, so I was in a real state. I mean, this was a real drama. So to avoid that whole problem, I took Derek back home as soon as possible to avoid something terrible taking place because the father was driving to the school to catch Derek. Fortunately I was able to reach the school in record time and get there before him.

Luckily the school explained the situation to the girl's father. At the end of the day, after the judge saw Derek and understood his situation, everything was well, the father understood and the injury wasn't bad. Phew; that was a close call.

"Every month I was waiting for a call from the school complaining about Derek, so I would have to chat with him to try and put him on the right track." I would have to be really strict with him because I was worried the school would ban him because he was too crazy. This was a very stressful time for my family and me. I never knew what would happen next. I was trying to be protective of Derek, but at the same time instill some discipline into him."

Overcoming adversity

There were many dramas while I was at school. I remember there was quite of lot of bullying I encountered during those years. I know it goes on all the time, but being blind didn't help. In fact bullying is a terrible thing, particularly for those children who have a disability. Yes, people would bully me because I was blind. Sadly, they thought I wasn't as smart as they were because I couldn't see. People would get so mad because as I walked, I would bump into chairs or people and the people would punch me. I certainly couldn't help it; I just couldn't see. But to be fair, I guess they didn't know this. It was so hurtful and also so embarrassing, definitely if others were around to witness this. I was very vulnerable and it's not a good way to be. Vulnerability can cause many negative feelings and thoughts.

I had a few friends, but when I had homework or assignments in groups, many students would try to cut me out because I was blind. If there happened to be a test with a pair working together, they would not want to work with me. Unfortunately, I just had to go through this. I had to overcome and there were many lessons to be learnt, good and bad. But I guess this put me in good stead for my coming years. Life was not going to be very easy for me and I had to overcome a lot to accomplish what my dreams were revealing to me – what was really stirring up in my heart.

My father said, "I was thinking about my emotions regarding bullying, particularly where Derek was concerned. It's a good subject to think about. Since Derek was three years old, I started to talk to him about bullying because I knew that would come up one day. Derek actually went a long way dealing with this. He did quite well.

"One day, when he arrived home, he was really sad and he told me the students were bullying him and named him 'little blind'. Then I sat down with him and said, 'Hey, you're blind and you're little and they are really saying the truth. You should also give them a nickname. So what goes forward comes back. They are bullying, but are saying the truth, so you can give them a nickname. If it's bullying about only making fun of people, just go with the flow. If you're big and fat, just go with this. If they are skinny, just go with the flow. Accept the truth and try and speak up and make people feel the same thing you are feeling. But if it's physical bullying, getting hurt or frightful words that hurt, then the family and friends should get together and try to help. The principal should also be informed.'

"Bullying is very difficult to deal with. I don't remember Derek complaining about too many bullying incidents. On the street, people were often mean to him because he would often unintentionally bump into them, but Derek and I would come to an understanding of this."

The stick
Up to about eight years of age, I didn't use a walking stick, but I was bumping into so many things. At the age of between eight to ten years, I had to use a walking stick, but I was very embarrassed to use this. It was a challenge that I had to go through; just another thing to deal with. Every blind child has to do a mobility course. I did this and I would hide my walking stick, which I could fold and hide in my pocket. Yes, I was a bit devious, but I also had some pride. Actually, the walking stick could

protect me, but I still bumped into everything. I would find all these bumps on my head. I wonder why?

I didn't really want to bring my walking stick to school. I felt very uncomfortable and it brought attention to myself in a negative way. I wanted my peers to think well of me and to include me in activities, but with a walking stick… Well, it was not a good look.

The first time I brought the stick to school, I was so embarrassed. Every student was looking at me. They were laughing and whispering, saying, "The little boy has a 'tree stick," so I was embarrassed. Hey, I was a young man in my own right and I wanted the respect and acceptance of the other students. Every young person wants that, and just because I was blind… After a few months, I got used to that and I didn't care too much, but it still hurt me. However, I overcame that bad situation and I had to accept who I was. I just had to face that. I don't go anywhere without my stick now. It is my eyes.

As I grew up, I made a decision that I wouldn't bring the stick with me. I knew where everything was at the school – it was like home. So why bother? But there was a time when they removed my classroom to another spot, as they were making the building larger. Unfortunately, I had to bring the stick with me because everything had changed and I couldn't find my way around unfamiliar territory. I also wanted more freedom and I couldn't always have someone to hold my hand. I was definitely too cool for that!

"So Derek, most of the time, could deal with that: the bullying and the mocking and having to use a walking stick. I told him to just go along with it all, but I felt really bad because I was unable to step in front of him and help him. I couldn't protect him. I couldn't go and correct the kids because they complained about my son playing pranks, but he never bullied them. As a father, this is what I wanted to do."

My father tried to protect and prepare me as much as he could because people always tried to make fun of me. His advice was always so good. After a while, I didn't care too much if they called me any nicknames. I suppose I got used to it and toughened up. But it was traumatic. No child wants to have to cope with this.

Run-ins with the bully
One day that we were playing at school with all of my colleagues and another student said to the school director that I made the floor dirty. I couldn't remember exactly what it was, but that was not me who did this. It was in fact him. He said he would punch me if I told the manager he was the one who caused this. I was scared because he was much bigger. He was the main really mean guy in my class. This is what I had to deal with constantly. I was a pretty strong character, but this constant badgering was pretty hurtful and difficult to cope with.

There was a guy who, every time I would walk by him, would try and be very aggressive with me. He was totally disrespectful to me because I was blind. He didn't like me being around at all and he made this very clear. There were times when I had to stand my ground, but it was all a strengthening process for years to come.

Once, we were at the soccer field when I was about ten years old and boys were playing with the soccer ball. I was so passionate about soccer and would have loved to pursue the sport. Unfortunately for me, the boys intentionally kicked the ball really fast and the ball hit my stomach so hard that I could barely breathe. One of the boys was laughing and being mean and I felt so sad. I was much smaller than him. I couldn't go back to playing soccer, as they could scare me easily. I felt so low and hurt. I didn't know what to do. Wouldn't anyone be kind and helpful to me? The students treated me as if it was my fault I was blind. I didn't ask for this.

I tried to be smart and always do my schoolwork. I didn't like to read because I was slow and I would be bullied. If I was asked to read text in front of the class, it was difficult. I always tried to hide from having to read as I was embarrassed. My exams would have to in Braille or orally with the teacher. Sometimes I would go to blind assistance, where they would help me to present an article or material written over to Braille. Many times I would record in voice memos. When a test or exam came, I could not count on receiving much help with class colleagues. They were not there for me; they would not help me in any way. This made me miserable so there was no encouragement to study.

When the results of the exams came, I tried to stay very positive. Fortunately, I was very upbeat, even though many things distressed me. But nobody was going to keep me down. In my mind, I had too much going for me and nothing would stop me.

I was a lover of soccer at school and I still am. For the first six years of my life, I could see some colors and shapes, but I couldn't see properly. So I decided to try to play soccer. I figured out the noise that the ball would make on the grass. I tried this, but it was so hard. If the ball was in the air, I couldn't hear it, so I had to give this up, which was very disappointing. I tried many ball sports, but I was not good at any of them. I tried out for the Olympic Games at school, but nothing worked. That was disappointing. I couldn't do anything. I was not good enough at sport to play with my friends. This made me feel really disabled. I just couldn't join in.

I did have a few friends in primary and high school; real friends I still have contact with, but some boys were really mean. So my school days weren't all that enjoyable. I guess all this bullying made me strong and determined to forge ahead in life. I didn't know what I would do at that stage, although I did love the surf. But I was determined that nothing would hold me back. There were, of course, times when I wondered what would happen to me, but I think the fact I was so active and adventurous helped me through many tough times.

Middle school

In middle school I remember the only time I failed in one subject was in Maths. Normally I was good at Maths but this was my first time at middle school and it was challenging. The teacher was nice but sadly the students were not so friendly or helpful. I found it really hard. None of the students helped me pass in the next exam. They didn't want to give me any assistance at all. I don't know why? This created a great deal of stress during my school years. We had to hire a tutor for home to help me. I was greatly challenged but wonderfully I passed the next exam and I learnt a great deal. It was a tough year for me.

In middle and high school, I struggled a lot with language — with English. I had a bad teacher; she was not nice and she didn't care if I learnt or not, so I didn't bother learning. Isn't that normally what a student does? She was always sending letters to my parents. I learnt English after my twenties because I was travelling the world for surfing.

In high school, it got harder with my studies and the bullying kept persisting. The schoolwork was definitely harder. I had to cope with different students and different teachers all the time. I didn't like these years. A few teachers were nice and wanted to help me, and one or two are still friends today. I really don't know what is wrong with people who have to be like this. I know I was probably a handful, with my disability and my over-exuberance, but I was still a good guy who wanted to learn. I was still a human being. I really learnt the importance of treating people with respect and honor. Once again, these were things I had to overcome and yes, I was eventually able to do this.

Many times I was the 'fall guy'. I would be blamed because I couldn't defend myself. That made me want to try to change schools. I signed up with other schools, but they wouldn't accept me, so I had to stay at my school for the rest of my study time. Things were so bad that I didn't even go to my graduation in high school because my classmates were not nice to me; they were not my friends. That was disappointing.

High school and graduation

"Oh, what made me so emotional were the graduations at the end of the year," my father described with such sentiment. "There were a lot of emotional times from pre-school until middle school. I couldn't believe it. He was one of the smartest students in all of the classes. Until today, I cannot believe he went to the primary, middle and high school and he graduated. Wow, that was awesome. I was so proud of my son. Until today, when I see the graduation pictures, tears come into my eyes. There are a lot of emotions, especially for me, because I couldn't believe he would float with the school, and the school method of teaching was extremely hard. But Derek made it. He got through! I was so grateful to see my son going along the years and graduating, especially a child who has any physical disability. I cannot tell you how proud and excited I was and I am still so proud incredibly today. Derek achieved so much."

CHAPTER 5.

CONQUERING THE IMPOSSIBLE

I have always loved to be in the ocean ever since I can remember. This gave me a deep desire to be a surfer. Since I was given that boogie board, I have always loved being around the ocean, playing with the waves. I have such a passion; it has always been in my blood. I have something within me that is connected with the waves. This is what gives me such a craving to be a surfer. I can't help it.

Learning to surf
I was starting to become more and more captivated by the surf. A guy in my hometown had a surf school. When I was around 15, I decided I wanted to surf, but no one would teach me. Then this guy said there were some surfboards coming from overseas and he promised he would teach me. That made me the happiest boy in the world. I thought all my Christmases had come at once. Unfortunately, it didn't happen and I was so disappointed. This guy made a promise, but this didn't come true. At this time I was in high school. My father knew what happened with the disappointment and promised that he would give me a board.

My father also knew the type of boy I was and he understood my hyperactive personality and how much I really wanted to achieve. He knew of the pain that I suffered because I was so let down, but as always, we had an amazing relationship and he was always there for me, loving me and encouraging me.

My father explained this so well. "I realized my boy was a very responsible boy, but very bratty and playful. Since he was born, I have been buying him toys for fun: basketballs and soccer balls. However, when he was about 17, this was the first year of his life that I did not want to face that he could not do what other boys were succeeding in, so I persevered and tried to tell him that he could do such things. I would say, 'My son, you must insist that you can be great at something. It can take longer than normal, it may not be perfect, or maybe better than other people, but you can do it.' It is with many tears and emotions that I report this. There were so many times that I spoke these positive words to him.

"Derek already had a 5'9" surfboard given to him from a boy he met on the beach. It was new, with a cover and everything else that was required. One day, he persisted so much for me to go surfing with him and I couldn't, so he insisted on going alone. I advised him the tide was very low and on the first wave he could do some damage and get hurt and still break the board. So what happened? He broke the board."

Yes, my father had told me not to go, that I would break my board, and yes, it happened, just as he had predicted. Well, of course, as a typical teenager, I didn't listen to him and actually went to the beach because I wanted to stand up on my surfboard. Although being blind, it was not a good idea. Really, what was I thinking? How did I expect to do this?

The first wave I paddled onto, I fell off and the board broke in half. Then I was very disappointed, so my father was naturally very mad and with good reason because I didn't listen to him. When would I learn?

So, for one year, I couldn't surf because I didn't have a board and I sadly had to put my surfing to the side. I lost some interest, but the desire to be a surfer was still in my heart. It wouldn't go away… I fought it with all my might, but no, it was there to stay. I really and truly wanted to go back to surfing.

The greatest gift
My father said, "When Derek was 17 I purchased some surfboards to sell at my store, but one of them I kept and I gave this to him as a present. I always tried to encourage him to do things, even though he could not see. I say those things with tears coming out of my eyes when I remember the moment I gave him the surfboard. It was such a special time.

"So I purchased a few more boards from the store and I gave him a 9-foot board, which was specially reserved for Derek so we would go surfing and have a lot of great fun together."

Dad took me to the ocean and he explained a few things. Then my first day at trying to surf, I didn't learn very much at all. Dad was expecting me to stand on the board straight away, as he did when he was 14, but for me, it was hard, very hard. Then I attempted to stand up again, but I didn't do that well. It was very difficult. I was wondering why I couldn't get it at first. I knew I was very bright, but then again, I couldn't see, so what could I expect?

After this, my father then told me that he was going to teach me how to surf. That was one of the greatest days in my life. I was so happy; that was amazing. He said to me, "You're going to be a surfer. I am going to take you to the water." I was really excited. Finally, I was going to learn to surf properly and with my father. Wow, that was so cool. He took me to the ocean; it was the first time surfing with him on a real surfboard. I was trying to stand up and he was really happy. He was cheering for me and showing me how to do things. We were having so much fun. We were the happiest son and father together. It was amazing. We would go often, as much as we could. It was nearly every day.

"A few months later, after I acquired the long 9-foot rim and was waiting for a perfect sea condition to teach Derek, he kept calling me every day," my father said. "But besides the sea being bad, I had a strong ankle twist and a cut underneath the big toe."

One day, when my father's foot was recovered, he said to me, "Good, today is the day that if you don't stand up on the wave, you are a terrible surfer." Yes, he was making light of this. "Derek never was afraid of the bigger waves. When he was young, I would take him out in the ocean to duck the big waves and surf on his boogie board," he recalled.

However, this did not last very long. One day, my father went to play soccer and then he came home with an incredibly bad injury to his knee. He couldn't walk he had to lie on the bed, with ice being applied to his knee and also take medications. When I saw he was like this, my first thought was, *Who am I going to surf with? Who is going to take me out surfing and have fun with me?* I was extremely annoyed and sad that he injured his knee because I couldn't surf with anyone. Later on I thought to myself, *I'm so selfish, I should be thinking that my Dad had a serious injury. I shouldn't be thinking about myself. I should be looking after his needs and praying'*.

Where there's a will...

One time, my uncle took me with my cousin to the beach and that was also a disaster. Another one. My uncle tried to help. It was good of him, but I just couldn't manage it. How frustrating that was. I am sure my uncle would have been disappointed. So that was the end of the adventure for a while. I had my surfboard at home and my uncle was telling me to go on my own, but I was scared, I wasn't confident enough.

We had a family friend, 'Pitbull', who my parents had known him for a long time and I also knew him since I was very young. He was a homeless man. He lived on the street and all he had was a little cart where he could carry his recycled items to sell so he could buy some food. He was a really happy guy. When my Dad was injured, I was trying to find a solution in every single way so I could keep surfing. Yes, I was very desperate to get into the water as much as I could. So that friend ended up going to the ocean with me a few times. He did not surf, but he swam really well, so he would be there for me to encourage and cheer for me. He was such a great friend to me. I appreciated the effort he made to take me to the beach.

Pitbull would make everyone laugh, so we loved his character. There was a time when he was living in the backyard of my grandmother's house, but it wasn't for long, as she had a few apartments rented out and the renters didn't want to have a homeless person hanging out in the backyard. This was sad for him and I felt so sorry that he was treated this way.

Another time when I was younger, my father had a store that was closed and he let Pitbull live there for a number of years. There were many times when Pitbull would share a meal with us. He loved it when my father cooked seafood. Until this day, I have a great relationship with him. I always help him as much as I can, especially because I know that he does not drink or use drugs. Every single coin that he was given would be used to feed himself.

Surf school
A few months later, after I hadn't surfed for a while, I was on the beach with my cousin and there were many people with surfboards. I could hear them talking about the surf. This, of course, got me very interested

and I listened to them very intently. Then I asked, "What's going on here?"

And they said, "It's a surf school."

I asked them, "Would you guys take me out in the ocean to learn to surf?"

They said they would have to ask their manager, as they didn't know if they would be allowed to take on this responsibility. I said, "Cool, please let me know." So they went to talk to him and came back to say they were allowed to take me out and would teach me how to surf. I was so excited. I went home and told my father that I found a surf school. I asked him, "Can you please sign me up so I can take some lessons."

Then he replied, "Of course not." I asked him why he wouldn't do this. He just said he would not give me the money to go to the surf school. He said to me, "You have learnt the basics. You live near the beach. Just jump into the waves and do it yourself because I have taught you a little bit."

I argued back, "I'm not brave enough. I'm blind; it is too hard."

My father said strongly, "You can make it, you can stand up on the board and have fun."

So after that, I was really upset. I ran to my mother because she sometimes said yes to my requests! I said, "Mom, I want to learn how to surf."

She replied, "Are you serious? Are you kidding me?" But I told her I was serious and that my father couldn't take me anymore and I needed someone to take me, otherwise I just would not learn. She asked me, "What did your father say?" I explained that I wasn't allowed to do it; he wouldn't give me the money.

Then my mother explained, "I'm not sure if I can go against your father's decision."

I said, pleading with her, "Mom, please do it for me." I was desperate. Well, I got my way. She gave me the money for the first month and signed the form for permission to learn. Then we agreed not to tell my father because it wouldn't go well for me.

So for the first month, I went to the surf school without my father knowing. In the first class, the teacher received me warmly. Everyone was so nice. He was teaching me well and he was really nice and patient with me. Every technique he knew for teaching his pupils he made sure he would pass it to me so I could feel it, hear it and touch all he taught me. My development was going so well because I had a great surf teacher. He was so patient and I had lessons twice a week. It was so much fun, I loved it. But what of my father? I was developing quickly and people were extremely impressed, even my mother. But my father still didn't know anything. I felt just a little guilty that he didn't know.

When he found out that I was in the surf school, he was really mad because he felt I didn't respect him. Someone told him, "Hey, your son is surfing really well. He's developing quickly."

He inquired, "What are you talking about? He's not surfing."

They replied, "Yes, at the surf school around the corner every week." Oops! My father was so angry he wanted to go and bring me home. He went to the surf school determined to get me away, but when he got there to bring me home and give me a punishment, his mind was blown out because he saw me getting a wave. *Oh, such great timing,* I thought. I was doing incredibly well. So he was speechless and full of joy to see his child doing so well in a short time. Phew, that was close. I knew I had disrespected him and I had felt bad about this, but what could I do? Surfing was in me.

I kept going every week and built a nice relationship with the surf teacher. He was not only teaching me how to surf; I was also developing in myself. I would go and surf with him sometimes when the waves were not that big. It was wonderful: feeling the water, feeling the wind in my face and standing up on the board. This was heaven at its best, and best of all, to have a teacher who was patient and kind and who could see potential in me.

My father continued to say, "Later on, I felt so bad I had to tell Derek that I didn't have the money to pay for the surf school, as my financial situation was already bad. Poor thing. He left all sad and downcast, but I didn't want to upset him about the money situation. However, he cleverly asked his mother to pay.

"The school was run by a man who says that when Derek told him that he wanted to learn to surf, he was amazed. He thought to himself, 'How will a blind boy learn to surf? There is no way!' But he did not say no to the boy. Already in the first few classes they became great friends. Derek would wake up early in the weekends and holidays to help set up the little school. He was so enthusiastic. Soon they were going to surf together in other beaches and formed a great friendship and partnership. This man is such a great guy for helping Derek with his surfing. I was very grateful."

A few months later when I was surfing, I got another good surfboard and then I went surfing again. It was the only surfboard that I had, but it broke and it was a great surfing day, but the waves were really heavy. Unfortunately, my surfboard broke in half. It got snapped by a wave. Then I was really heartbroken and crying on the beach because I didn't have a board to ride. I had to save a bit of money to try and buy another one, but I did this and later I got a new board and kept surfing. So all was good.

Magno

I want to tell you about the time I met a great friend, Magno. He is someone I am so grateful for and will never forget. He has made such an impact on my life, particularly in the area of my surfing. My father tells the story. "As Derek was reaching the age of about 17, there was a time in his life that he was starting to go out with friends and colleagues, more his college friends and neighbors and all the friends he met along the way. I was wondering what influence they would have on Derek's life. This is something every parent thinks about, I'm sure. Even though they were good people, they were not Christian. I asked Derek, 'Why don't you go out more often with friends from the church?'

"Derek answered, 'I'm not sure.' Derek was going out and partying at night, doing nothing wrong, but as fathers we always worry when your child starts to go out and they get home late. I don't think I am alone in this concern.

"One day I was in front of my store and a friend of mine came to talk to me. His name was Magno. We were just chatting in front of the store on the beach walk and he also had his little child with him. I introduced him to Derek. I said, 'Derek this is Magno, he is a boogie board champion. He surfs really well; he's one of the Top 10 in the world. He is a champion and also a hero for our home town.'

"Then Derek said, 'Oh cool.' After Magno left, I said to Derek, 'Hey, do you remember me saying to you that you should watch who you hang with?' and Derek said, 'Yes.' Then I said, 'Magno is a perfect example of someone to hang out with. He's a great guy. He has a good character and a good heart. He surfs really, really well. He's not a guy who will do crazy parties and he is a Christian he loves the Lord.' That's what I told Derek. Then a few months later, naturally they started to hang out together. They started to be friends and get some waves together and became closer. They actually became best friends.

"That made me really happy because I knew my child was hanging out with someone really nice. Magno had a huge impact on Derek's life because he started to be his surf coach and prepare him for better waves. Also, he had an impact in terms of chasing and seeking the path of Christ, so they are great friends until this day."

During our time together as friends, we would just hang out at my hometown, going to church and spending time together. We would have breakfast and lunch and enjoy each other's company. We would also get a lot of waves surfing. Magno would help me to push myself beyond my limits. I improved my surfing a lot after I met him even though he was a boogie boarder.

Magno said, "When I first met Derek, he was very brave being blind and surfing. I thought to myself, 'This man is crazy, I have to spend some time with him.' Back then, I was a professional body boarder. I thought he could teach me some things. Some days we went surfing in the dark so I could experience what it was like for him."

I remember once we were on a trip to get some waves near my hometown and we had to go through the bush to get to the beach. It was a secret spot. It was so secretive that we got thoroughly lost! It was kind of like a trail. We were so lost and disappointed because we knew we only had a short window of opportunity to get the great waves.

We were thinking that an amazing surfing session that morning had vanished. That was not a good start, especially to a surfer, but then we began to pray and we started to feel the presence of the Holy Spirit. That was an amazing experience with God. We were in the middle of nowhere without food, water and more importantly, without waves! But we were so happy and we found the presence of God, and we didn't care any more about the waves. We knew that we were missing one of the best days of surfing of that year, but after we prayed, the wind was blowing very strongly and we knew that the waves would not be that good any more; they would be really bumpy and closing out. Then we immediately found the way to the beach. It was God's miracle, right after praying. Just to think that God is interested in every aspect of our lives is wonderful.

So we eventually made our way to the beach. The waves were terrible; they were not good anymore. Very messy, closing out and small. There was no chance to surf any more. We were so exhausted and we still wanted to get wet because it was a really hot day. So we were saying, 'Let's jump in the water, let's just get wet.' Even though the surf was really bad, I got a wave and it was amazing, unbelievable. God blessed me with a really good wave on that day. I was so thankful.

"After I got out of the water, a photographer came to me and told me he got a really nice picture of me. I had no idea that someone was photographing me. The next morning that picture of me on that wave was in the newspaper, with an article about me. It is really wonderful how God does things. I didn't know at the time that this was a sign of things to come. It is amazing: we had been so disillusioned because we had lost a whole morning of waves, but with one single wave, God gave me an amazing picture. It was a nice article about me on the Internet the next morning. So that was really cool.

Pipeline

One day, Magno dreamt that I was getting really famous. Pictures of me were in many surfing magazines, websites and TV channels. The whole world knew about the blind surfer and also God was healing my eyes so I could tell people how great our God is. So every year, Magno would go to Hawaii to compete in the world contest at Pipeline. He was always telling me how good Pipeline is, so naturally this got me thinking. Something was stirring within me. I started to ponder life outside of Brazil. I realized I wanted to go to Hawaii and surf. This is what I would aim for. Magno set me on a course for my life that would prove to be my destiny.

    I wasn't about to give up on the idea of conquering this sport; conquering the power and splendor of the waves. By now, it was 'in my blood', but I had a great deal of overcoming to do to move forward and achieve what was in my heart.

CHAPTER 6.

MY GOAL – COLLEGE OR SURF?

I knew I had to work and do something with my life, but the surf was always calling me. My whole focus was on catching waves, so what was I to do? You have probably guessed which decision I made!

After I left my high school, I was not sure what I wanted to do. I hadn't given this too much thought while I was studying. I guess my whole focus was on surfing and because I was so hyperactive, this sport kept me very energized. But I knew I had to refocus and think of my studies. At some point, I thought I would study law and then I thought of chemical engineering and I just knew I could excel at these professions, even though I was blind. I would find a way. However, these two career paths I didn't feel at peace about. I just wasn't sure. I couldn't get the idea of surfing for my career out of my head, although this didn't seem feasible at the time.

Then I considered something in the area of fitness and training, but that is too broad a subject and I didn't know which way to go with this. It was a big decision and one that I had to think carefully about, but surfing wouldn't leave my heart and mind. It was there constantly, harassing and drawing me to come closer and be more involved. It was foremost in my heart and mind. What to do when you are being drawn in a certain way?

My heart was calling out to me. Therefore, my desire to surf more was becoming stronger, so it did make it more difficult to make a decision about my future.

An opportunity
When I finished high school and I was thinking hard about what to do, an opportunity was presented to me. The opportunity was with a huge international company, where they would pay the successful candidates to study, if approved in a selection process. The course was in environmental management and I liked the idea of doing this. It was something I could be happy with. I have always been interested in the environment. I think as a surfer, being out in the water, you become aware of nature, so I thought this was a great idea. Not only would my studies be paid for, but I would also be paid while studying. I got really excited by this proposition. This sat right with me.

So I signed up to do the test. There were one thousand people chasing this same opportunity, as of course, everyone wanted the chance. It was also advertised everywhere. When the test and course were finished, they would hire five or ten of the best students with the best grades so they would have a good job. *Wow, this would be a great opportunity,* I thought to myself.

The exam was so hard; I didn't know if I would make the grade. However, wonderful news. I got approved. From 0-10, the score I got was 7.8. I was on the limit, but it didn't matter. At least I was in. I was in the first 40 best grades out of 1000. How amazing was that? And I was blind! So I started to study. Everyone on that course was very nice and they all encouraged me. The teachers were great too. What a relief... so different to my school days.

I had to go on the bus every day, but then I met someone who I became friendly with and I travelled to college in his car with him. This was very convenient and saved me a lot of time. The travelling on the bus was very frustrating and not every passenger was obliging. They wouldn't offer me a seat, even knowing that I was blind. I just had to accept this.

However, when I was studying, I was always surfing. I couldn't get it out of my system. No way... I knew surfing was in my blood. I felt I was made for this sport, but what to do? I was blind and I didn't think I could make a career out of surfing. I may have been wrong in thinking this at the time, but I was just looking at the facts and the physical side to my life. I didn't fully consider what Almighty God could do with me.

Sometimes, the afternoon would be a good time to study, as well as on the weekend. I would go to a friend's house to study and do assignments, but the surf was calling me. It was always calling me. Also some projects were tough, as I couldn't see. This was difficult. I was not as close to God as I was meant to be, so that was something that took me out of the track of school and out of focus with everything. By the end of the year, I was presenting the last project and there was a lot of work to do to graduate.

When I completed the course, I went to the graduation of the college. The students and I had always gone to parties together and always studied together – it was a wonderful time of my life. I will never forget that. I loved this time because I was accepted and respected for who I was. I think this was the first time that I experienced this acceptance in my school days and I really appreciated it. It was a very special time for me.

Decisions, decisions

The company that funded the course opened up an exam to hire some people. They would hire some of the best students in the class to work.

They would get the best five or 10 in the class. I was included in that selection. Wow, I was really happy. I was not really expecting this, but it was so cool. At the same time in that year, I was planning my first trip to Hawaii with my friend Magno to go surfing. So I wanted to go to Hawaii, but I knew I had received the opportunity of my life for work. I didn't really have money to go to Hawaii then, so I thought I would go later. No one else had wanted to take a blind surfer to Hawaii, but my friend had wanted to. Then I had to make a really huge decision: I go to Hawaii, or apply for the job. Either make surfing just my hobby, or I lose this opportunity, or then again lose the dream of surfing in Hawaii.

My final decision was to go to Hawaii. I turned down the opportunity for work. I just wanted to have fun. I didn't care about anything else. By that time, I was so into surfing and I was not thinking about leaving my favorite sport. I just wanted to surf, that's all I wanted to do. Sometimes, little thoughts of being a professional surfer would often come to me and at that moment, I remembered something my uncle told me, which was actually true. He said, "Derek, make sure you study a lot because it's not easy to be a professional surfer. A career of a professional surfer… well, it is really hard to live a life with surfing." He was right. Many people try and they are not successful. I was at college when he told me that and I took on board what he said. I wanted to study, but my heart was definitely elsewhere.

Thankfully I made a wise decision, and I did pursue my surfing. It was probably not the best decision I could recommend to everyone, but I knew God had His favor upon me and I was blessed. I went to Hawaii and turned everything around. My whole life changed. It was sensational in Hawaii, I must admit. Firstly, to get to Hawaii was a great mission. I was told I was crazy. Everyone said this: family, friends, teachers. But I knew I was on a quest. I didn't have any money at the time. My parent's business was not good, but some of my friends helped me. I just wanted to be there and get some waves. That's all I could think about.

There was so much opposition; people telling me not to go, that I would die. But my friend, Magno, was encouraging me to go. He said, "You can make it, you're a good surfer." So we worked hard, getting prepared and training. I am so grateful to Magno for all his support and encouragement. He has made such an impact on my life and helped me make my ultimate decision.

I could have gone either way. My life could have been very different if I had chosen work. I would not be writing a book; I would instead be writing a report about a bushfire or pollution in the ocean. This was a significant time in my life. But I had a dream! I wanted to go to Hawaii to surf. There have been many challenges in my life, but I never let any of them stop me from moving forward because I believe that God can do great things for those who believe in Him.

CHAPTER 7.

HAWAII – MY PIPELINE DREAM

I was finally going to fulfill my vision of going to Hawaii. I was so excited; I couldn't believe this was happening. It was a real step of faith for me, but I did it! It was like a dream come true. This had been my desire for so long.

My father remembered, "When Derek started to tell me ideas about Hawaii, that started to make me realize that Hawaii is very dangerous and a few people have had bad accidents and been badly injured. I didn't have money to help him with his trip. I was going through a really hard time with my business. I was broken and I was really embarrassed not to be able to help my child. I was happy for him, as this was his dream. I didn't want to stop him from doing it. I just let him stay with his dream, without saying anything. I thought the idea would not be that serious, but I started to believe this more when he told me that he was going to go to Hawaii with Magno, who is someone I was very impressed with.

When he told me he was going to apply for his passport I thought, 'Well I guess my son is actually going to Hawaii – I cannot do much.' I came to him and said, 'Hey Derek, you know I don't have money to help you. How are you going to do it?'

"He was a bit sad to hear that, but it was the truth. I had to share the

HAWAII – MY PIPELINE DREAM

truth with him, but I didn't want to take his hope away from him. He felt a bit hopeless, but he started to work on it. He used to have a few surfboards that he would get from other people – very old surfboards. He would re-sell them and started to make some money with those business transactions and other surf gear that he would acquire.

Making the dream a reality
"He would get these from little companies that would give him free stock: leg ropes, surf wax and so on. So he started to put all those things together and sell them so he could save money to go to Hawaii. Also, his mother rented out her house and she gave him part of the money to help with his travels and buy the tickets. When I saw all those things happening, and knowing I couldn't help my child, I was a bit frustrated. I didn't know what to do. I just wanted to be the best father. I saw that my child was looking forward to going to Hawaii and he was doing his best. With all of those challenges and problems he had to face, he didn't give up on his dream of going there.

"One of my friends owned a surf shop in our home town and I told him that Derek was going to Hawaii. He did not have a big company, but he pulled up some money and said, 'Give that to Derek, that will help him to buy some snacks and food – at least at the beginning of the trip.' So all of that together was a gift from God and started to encourage Derek to go to Hawaii."

Getting ready for the trip was a challenge in itself, to say the least. I had no money, but I had a great friend who really believed in me and all that I wanted to achieve. It was a really hard time, but at the same time exciting. I just wanted to make my dream come true. So the time arrived when I was to finally get on the plane to go to Hawaii. I had never been on an airplane before. Everything was really weird and terrifying for me.

I was a bit scared. I didn't understand much at all of what was happening. I couldn't see or comprehend the enormity of flying. Everything was really challenging. I spoke no English. I didn't even know how to order my own food on the plane. It was so dramatic that I thought I never wanted to fly anywhere again. Little did I know…

When I finally arrived in Hawaii, after the ordeal of flying I was so thrilled to be there. This was my dream place. I was so excited that I forgot my backpack and left it outside of the airport on the ground, with all my valuable possessions in it. I mean everything! Passport, visa, money… I realised that I forgot it only when I was at the house that I was staying in. Fortunately, I was able to retrieve it all. Someone found it and left it inside the airport. All was not lost. Not a good beginning, but I didn't care. I had landed. All I kept thinking was, *Great tomorrow I'm going to surf.*

I naturally thought it would be easy to just turn up and surf. I mean, isn't Hawaii supposed to be the ultimate? Everything I had heard was this was the greatest place on earth to catch awesome waves. However, the biggest problem was there were too many people trying to surf at the same spot. Hawaii is a place everyone wants to go to surf. It is the ultimate, but it is also so very challenging. However, I must admit that at first it felt like I surfed with a group of men who had, by nature, gifts that seemed superior to mine.

Sadly I was a little disillusioned at first. I didn't expect to come face to face with the huge crowds of surfers, but I suppose if a place is so well known and everyone wants to surf there… well… what did I expect? Maybe I didn't think this through enough? Anyway, I was here in my dream place. That's all that mattered. When I arrived in Hawaii, I had the feeling there was something different there. I was valuing a really beautiful place, without seeing it. I was trying to appreciate as much as

I could just by hearing, by listening, by feeling and by touching things in that amazing place. I knew there was something special between Hawaii and me. I felt it was something I longed for all my life.

I felt I was in another world; the world of my dreams. I would appreciate every single little item that I could grab and bring to my own world inside of my mind. The first time I went to the beach, I was slowly walking so I could feel the sand around my feet. I could feel the breeze of the ocean. I could feel the power of the rainbows. I could feel the salty air blowing around my face. I could also feel when I was surfing. It was important to touch the rocks, the reefs. It was cool to touch nature as much as I could to touch the house where I was staying. To touch the plants, the flowers. I really wanted to make sure that I could have the image of Hawaii in my mind as close as possible to what it really is.

I made it
The first day I was in Hawaii, I went to surf at Pipeline, which is the highlight for any surfer. It was so wonderful to be there. I remember I didn't sleep at all the night before; I was so worried. I knew it was a huge and dangerous beach and many people try to surf there at the same time, so this creates another hazard. I was so nervous, I couldn't concentrate, but I was enthusiastic and happy at the same time. I pictured myself riding the waves and getting barreled. I was seeing all that in my mind. I was surfing Pipeline!

I remember a year before I went to Hawaii. One night, I dreamt I was surfing at Pipeline. In my dreams I can see things. I can physically see things the way I imagined them to be. For example, what a car looks like. Well, there are four wheels, the car may be blue and the car is made from iron. I can create a picture in my mind. That is so incredible. I love that sensory perception that has been given to me.

Well, that night I dreamt I was getting great waves and it was a beautiful day. I remembered that dream and said to myself, *tomorrow is going to be my dream day the way I actually dreamt it to be.* Unfortunately, it didn't happen that way and I was so disappointed. When I got there, the surf was different. I didn't get any decent waves. It was totally the opposite to what I had imagined it to be. I was very disillusioned. My friend Magno was encouraging me, saying, "That's how it is in Hawaii: everyone is trying to do the same thing." It didn't help very much. We kept trying each day. Then it started to become easier and I knew this is what I had dreamt. It was becoming more exciting.

My father explained the situation. "Once Derek arrived in Hawaii, all of those challenges that happened prior to his departure were making him upset in the beginning. But once he arrived, he just kept going and persevering and he met the locals. I had always warned him to respect them because there are a lot of respectful things that are part of the Hawaiian culture. He made many friends."

So many people have died surfing at Pipeline, but even though I knew this, it didn't stop my dream of getting some waves. It was still the place for my dream waves. Pipeline has one of the most amazing barrels on the whole planet. It has perfect waves, but little mistakes made can create some really serious accidents. The second day I was in Hawaii, there were no waves at all, but we were quite sure that the following day there would be good waves.

Unfortunately, when I woke up the next morning I was very sick. I had a really bad fever with a bad throat and headache. It was not what I had expected. I couldn't surf. I was actually sick for about five days. I just couldn't get out of bed, so I missed five days of good waves. I was very disappointed because I knew there were good waves pumping. Not a good start. As always, challenges were being fired at me, but I was

HAWAII – MY PIPELINE DREAM

getting stronger.

Finally, I was free from my infirmity and I could prepare to get some great waves. I knew that the surf was going to be really, really good. I also knew the waves would be big, but that would be a lot of fun. I didn't sleep that well the night before my big adventure. I was extremely impatient and excited, thinking all the time about surfing. I was imagining myself getting those waves as I had dreamt about when I was sleeping one year ago.

So Magno and I went to the beach. I put the legrope on my surfboard, waxed it well and jumped in the water. We prayed as always before we hit the ocean. My thoughts were like, *this is amazing I am in paradise. I am where most of the surfers want to be one-day. I'm here in front of Pipeline, but I'm blind.*

Actually, I was just a surfer having fun. It was different to all those professional surfers around with sponsors and being paid to get waves. I was thinking it was amazing that some people get paid to do what they love doing. I was starting to reflect...

Magno and I leapt into the water and we paddled towards the outside where the waves were. I tried to get waves all the time, but I couldn't. Any time that I would try to catch a wave, it turned out to be impossible. There would always be someone else, or a number of surfers on the wave. That's just the way it is.

It's really crowded at Pipeline.

Needless to say, that made my life really difficult and frustrating. I was there in the water for two hours and I didn't get any waves. I was really disappointed because we fought so hard to get to Hawaii.

I was so stoked to think I could possibly get some waves on the next day. Unfortunately, there were no waves on that day; it was really flat. So I was just hanging out around the island. However, I noticed that other people were getting good waves, even Magno. I was trying to understand the purpose of God. Why did He take me to Hawaii? I was thinking to myself, *I am here for a week and not surfing. There are no waves. I lost my backpack and then I was sick. Why am I here?* I couldn't quite understand all this, but I still believed that the best was to come. Some good waves were going to break at Pipeline the following day. Magno told me to be prepared, that tomorrow is the day.

I was preparing my surfboard and remembering that a few years before, I dreamt that one day I was going to be at Pipeline. I dreamt I was getting great waves and barrels, so the day came and we went to Pipeline early in the morning. We were at the beach at 7 a.m. The surf was pumping. I was so excited; I felt like I was a little kid in the playground, but in my mind I was expecting only good things would happen on that day. We paddled out and there was a guy with a camera who was supposed to film us. Once we paddled along the channel in the water, I realized how many people were there. I could hear them talking about the waves. There were so many people chasing for the same waves. Imagine a room with maybe 50 hungry dogs chasing the same bone. That's what it felt like.

I waited patiently for my turn. I tried to get one wave. I paddled for that wave, but somehow I couldn't get it. I tried another time to get another wave the same morning but there was already someone who owned it. This kept happening and I was so frustrated.

We were in the water more than one hour and I thought, *This is not for me. How am I going to do this?* There were just so many people and the locals here get every single wave. There are many pro-surfers there who are so good and I am just a blind surfer. I didn't think I could manage it. I didn't think I could get those waves. So those things were getting into my heart, making me feel sad. I started to lose confidence and that concerned me. The fear and the feeling of giving up was surrounding me and trying to put me down. It would not let me pursue my dream. What was I going to do? This was not how I imagined my holiday to be.

When I was out in the ocean, something positive happened. Magno tried to position me really close where the barrels of Pipeline break were so I could feel the power of the ocean and also feel how heavy and how loud a barrel breaking at Pipeline is. I could also taste the saltwater as the barrels were breaking and spray was coming out of the barrels. That moment was a highlight because I got to experience the power of a Pipeline barrel.

When I came out of the water, I sat on the beach and I could tell Magno was upset as well because he saw me in that state. So, we didn't know what to do. We were so disappointed, but God kept that light of the joy and the miracle in our hearts and Magno came to me and said, "Derek, God brought us here. Let's pray and He will open the doors."

Friends in high places
Even though I was disappointed. I looked at him and said, "Well, let's do it," so we went to the church he had visited before in Hawaii. We also met some amazing people there. God greatly opened doors. I met amazing people there who were friends with the greatest surfers of Hawaii. They introduced me to those surfers who believed in me and with open arms received me as their family.

After going to the church, I went to the Brazilian church on the North Shore of Hawaii. Through Bruno Lemmos, I was able to meet big wave legend named Eddie Rothman and his son. I was really well received at their house. The first time I met Eddie, he said, "Hey I want to meet you. You are such an inspiration." He gave me a hat. He said for me to stop by his house anytime, so I met other people at the church and they lived with Eddie and they told me that Eddie really wanted me to visit him at his house.

So I decided to visit him. I went there with Magno, but I knocked at the wrong house. Instead, I arrived at his son Macau's house. I had a Brazilian jersey with me and he said, "Wow, who are you? But whoever you are, you have a Brazilian jersey, so you are welcome." And then he mentioned the name of a Brazilian soccer player, Ronaldo, who is really well known. At that time, he didn't know I was a surfer.

Then I told him, "Your dad told me to come here." Then he called his father who said to bring me over to his home – that I was the blind surfer.

Macau was very surprised that I could surf. He said, "That's amazing you are a surfer. I'm going to bring you a hat." Then Makau went away and came back with a brand new surfboard. Makau asked me, "Why are you here in Hawaii?" Then I told him my dream was to surf at Hawaii, but it was being difficult. I couldn't get any waves. The locals in Hawaii have a really strong reputation, as they want to protect their turf. They want to make sure that everyone respects everyone else. They carry that identity with them. They want to make sure they get their waves – so they are protected. But the whole Rothman family was so kind to me. I appreciate everything they did for me.

Eddie Rothman commented. "I liked him because he is funny. He has such great faith. He was surfing, doing this and that. Derek was on his way: he was surfing and surfed Pipe. He was doing it – nothing was getting in his way. He already had the talent. He had his parents and friends to back him up. He was on his path already. It was so ingrained in him. I saw it coming. I just walked away. God already had him. He was doing what he was meant to do."

My father also explained about the Rothmans. "Finally, after some time in Hawaii, one of the friends Derek made was Eddie Rothman. Eddie is the owner of Da Hui, a clothing company with his son, Makua, and they received Derek as one of their family members. They are very powerful in Hawaii, as they are really great surfers and have lived there for a long time. They made sure Derek could get as many waves as he could and as many as he wanted. What happened with Derek over there was incredible because that has never happened with anyone else. Derek was surfing in the most wanted spot in the world because the locals who live in Hawaii and who have the final word were his friends."

Fortunately, the locals received me very well, as they have never done before with anyone else in Hawaii, outside of the renowned professional surfers. They took me to surf Pipeline, and when they got on the lineup on the outside where the wave breaks, they would speak to everyone in the water saying, "Here we have a blind surfer from Brazil . He can get any waves that he wants. Please don't get on his waves. No-one behind him in front of him – nowhere. It's all his. He will surf as much as he wants to." I was feeling the blessings from God over me.

I was so happy and blessed, but I felt nervous at the same time, knowing I was surfing Pipeline with Macau. From catching no waves on my trip, in one and a half hours, I got so many waves. It was just amazing for me. It was wonderful. I felt like I was in heaven. Looking back at the time I went to the Brazilian church in Hawaii had a big impact on my life. That was how I met Bruno Lemos. When Bruno saw me, he later told me that he thought, "This little boy is in Hawaii. What is he doing here, because he is blind and he can't even see how pretty Hawaii is? He can't even experience the beauty of Hawaii." When he heard I was there with the idea of surfing Pipeline, he just couldn't believe it.

Once I was taking off on the wave, I felt something huge: guidance from God driving me through that wave. I felt there was a party inside my heart, pumping inside my chest. I was feeling so blessed… I knew that if I surfed in Hawaii, I would have a chance that I could die. It's really that dangerous. I had to make a choice. It's not only about surfing the waves I want, but also learning to accomplish things, even though I am blind. I didn't let that stop me. So now, inspiring people is also a part of me being happy and to encourage people. I learnt a lot.

A taste of fame
While I was in Hawaii, the idea to do a movie was a serious thought. One day, while I was on the beach listening to the waves someone came up to me and asked me, "What if we do something serious about you, like a movie?"

I agreed and we did a video, a short documentary for Youtube, which reached many people around the world. In fact, one video has reached over nine million people. That is a lot of people who know about my faith.

I will never forget that day. My life was turned around on that beach. It resonated with me that I could do something more with surfing. At that time, surfing was not my job. I had a few sponsors for surfing accessories like leg ropes, but surfing was still just my hobby. One day, I was at Pipeline and we were walking through the parking lot. Bruno saw me walking at Pipeline and he said, "What are you doing here?"

And then I said, "I'm going to surf Pipeline."

Bruno said, "There's no way I'm going to miss this. I'll come back to film it." So Bruno came back and filmed me surfing. Another day, after we surfed with Macua and Bruno filmed me, he made me really famous in the surfing community. Half a million views on Youtube in one week. Wow, that was incredible.

After I finished surfing and filming with Bruno, he said, "Hey Derek, why don't we start to do a documentary? The real thing. Not a Youtube video, but let's shoot big and share the story of your life." That's how the idea of the movie started. Then we met Bryan Jennings, a surfer and filmmaker from San Diego, and he said he wanted to be involved with that. So we didn't have a script for the movie, but it's interesting to see it was written by God and where it ended up.

A miracle stay

The day I was to leave Hawaii, I was crying because I didn't want to go back home. I was having a great time meeting new people and surfing the waves of my dreams. However, it was time to go. The money was gone, as we had been there for about 40 days. We went to the airport to get the flight and I was crying. I just didn't want to leave. I was trying to check in and somehow my flight was not there! Somehow on the computer system, my booking was cancelled by mistake. So I couldn't believe it – my booking was cancelled! That was cool, I thought, as I could stay until they solved the problem. Apparently I was not going to fly on that day. But I had no money. What was I going to do?

Thankfully, friends from the Brazilian church helped me. They received me in their homes. We stayed there and I saw how amazing God was. I ended up staying two more weeks in Hawaii. Somehow, they had to change my flight and they could only book me two weeks later, so I had a further blessed time there.

Then my life started to turn around. While I was being filmed, people were coming up to me and were interested in what was going on. That was really cool. It was one of those 'suddenly' moments: everything was changing.

Bryan Jennings comments, "Derek has a dependency upon God that we all should have and his faith has aided him to achieve all he has done as a blind person. *How does he accomplish surfing?* many people would ask. He knows that God will protect him and bless him because he has seen it happen so often. Derek has exchanged fear for his faith in Jesus Christ."

I often look back and think about how I felt on the waves. I must admit that I felt like going further: getting a bigger and more challenging wave. I always like to challenge myself. I was starting to pay more attention to the surf world. All the professional surfers were making a living from it and I though to myself that this is something I could potentially achieve. However, I would need to take a different approach, as it is hard to be a professional surfer and have a sponsor when you are blind.

On that first trip, the desire to become a professional surfer was growing. A little seed was planted in my heart, but I still wanted to chase something bigger. Not just in the size of the waves, but a mission for something else.

CHAPTER 8.

A YOUNG STAR IS BORN

I was so excited the idea had come for a movie. That was such great news, however, it was a little scary at the same time. Imagine a young guy like me starring in a movie about my life. I wondered at the time if I was really worthy of this as I was only young. However I wanted to experience every situation that seemed to offer a chance of gaining the greater understanding that I wanted and would give glory to God.

At the beginning, the idea was for a short documentary. I was not too excited at first as I thought it wouldn't be anything too significant, but God started to turn this around to something far greater, as he loves to do. We started to film in 2012 and this ended up becoming a really great documentary about my life. Bruno Lemos, my photographer friend, had the initial idea and together with Bryan Jennings, we started to filming. Unfortunately, we didn't have enough resources and funds to produce the entire movie, but thankfully, Bryan Jennings, together with his ministry, started to raise money and it was so successful. God provided everything we needed to do the movie.

The main focus of this movie was the story about my journey to achieve my dream of surfing at Pipeline. That is what I had dreamt about for many years. Filming the movie was a huge experience in my life. There was a lot going on behind the scenes of the movie. For example when you watch the movie, you see the great things, but some of the stressed moments, some of the frustrating times, you naturally don't see.

Because of the movie I started to get sponsored by big surf brands and also some co-sponsors of other brands as well. They are big companies. During the filming, I was able to meet a lot of professional surfers like Tom Carroll, Kelly Slater and CJ Hopgood. I was able to surf with them and get advice from them, which was a wonderful experience.

One of the first frustrations with the movie was when we went to record a wave and I didn't get the barrel that I wanted. In fact, during the filming of the movie I didn't get a barrel at all. So that was a difficult result for the scene we wanted to shoot.

Behind the scenes, everything became a bit upsetting and frustrating. Filming for a movie sounds very glamorous and exciting, but, let me tell you, it is not necessarily so. It is very demanding and time consuming. But we kept filming regardless. This movie took over two years to complete. We filmed in Brazil, California and Hawaii. We also recorded powerful interviews with my family, friends and some surfer colleagues.

God gave us this script, the money, the right time. Everything was perfect. We were lost in the beginning; we didn't know what we would do with that movie. We definitely were novices! As I mentioned before, we were planning to do a short documentary, but God changed this to a long story and he brought the right people. In fact, everything we needed was supplied. That was a miracle in itself.

Behind the scenes, crazy things happened. There were little fights between people: like who is actually doing the movie? One minute of shooting takes about a week. You could film the whole day for just one or two seconds of the film.

For the two years of filming, we had so many things slowing us down. There was the decision of how to raise the money – of being in the right place at the right time with the right people. I didn't speak English at all when I was doing the movie. This was a huge challenge I had to go through. I had to communicate with people who didn't speak my language, which was Portuguese. In the movie, I spoke English. I had to memorize the whole narration about myself. Of course, I got the translation in Portuguese, but I was speaking English without knowing what the words really meant in Portuguese. That's why my English in the movie was quite bad: it was because I didn't know the language or what I was speaking. This was a really stressful part of the movie.

Another 'behind the scenes' incident is when Kelly Slater asked if I could get a barrel on the back of a boogie board at Pipeline, then he would surf Pipeline with me one day. We made it. I surfed at the back of body boarding legend Mark Stewart, so Kelly and I arranged to surf Pipeline together, just to get a shot for the movie.

As we were filming one of the last parts of the production, I was walking down the beach and I bumped into Kelly Slater. One of the team walked up to him and said, "Hey Kelly, can you just take Derek out and do this shot for the movie?"

Then Kelly said, "The waves are firing, it's just so good."

Then we asked him again and he said, "Okay, let's do it quickly." So there were some very difficult incidents behind the scenes.

All about Jesus

We were not just filming things by chance. Everything was pre-planned. But during the movie one of the most amazing things happened. I was already a Christian, but I was never baptized. When I was in Hawaii filming, I took that decision to really make my faith my own; to really give my life to Christ. I wanted to be baptized in the ocean in Hawaii at Pipeline. That was my desire. So, I was baptized and I really gave my life to Jesus. I made a real commitment to God and then I became a new man. We filmed that for the movie too.

During the baptism, one of the guys who was filming decided to give his life to Jesus, so he left the camera and he said, "Hey, I also want to follow this Jesus, this God who Derek follows. Can I also be baptized by your pastor?" He walked to the water and the pastor baptized him and he received Christ. That was a real highlight for me.

Inspiring others
During the recording. there was one thing that impacted my life and the lives of others. It was an ordinary script, but when the director and I were working, someone got in touch with us, saying that a particular couple had a baby and he was blind and he had some brain issues. He had had 11 surgeries on his brain. When one of the operations was taking place in the theater, and while the parents were waiting, they heard about me, so they watched one of my videos on the Internet. They then became hopeful when they saw there was a blind guy who could surf and had faith in God. They contacted us to let us know they had seen the video. I encouraged them through my faith in God.

We ended up interviewing the family for the movie. It was a huge impact on the whole of my story. I got to know the family and they had hope because of what God was doing in my life. Unfortunately, three years later the baby couldn't hold on to life any longer and he passed away. There were too many issues with his brain. This was a very sad time, but it left a huge impression in my life.

Another behind-the-scenes incident was when a couple was walking along the beach near my home and they were looking for me. They heard

I was doing a movie in my hometown and they knew my parents had a store on the beachfront. They asked a lady, "Where is the blind man's parent's store on the beach? My child has been so inspired by him and we want to meet him."

The lady said, "I think I know where it is." That lady was my mother, and when she was talking to the couple and telling them about me, she was so emotional and started to cry. I guess what had happened to me had brought a lot of memories and emotions back to her. My mother had remembered what I had been through.

The crew working on the movie involved a number of people. Everyone enjoyed doing this time, but on looking back, I think the enemy brought a lot of arguments between all of us. I am glad I didn't get caught up with any bad situations with anyone. I am still in touch with everyone, even if I am not as close as before. But between that crew I can tell that there was a lot of arguments, particularly between the director, the editor and between people who were involved in the filming of the movie. There was a lot of stress that came to the surface. Everyone was feeling the pressure and emotion of putting a film together. This is because many ideas were coming up at the same time that didn't match with those of other people, which I suppose was bound to happen. Everyone has a different point of view.

When we were recording, I could tell my friend and coach at the time was really homesick. He was missing his wife and kids and we were very far from home. He thought he would have my full attention, but I had many friends, so it couldn't happen.

Through all this there was a lesson I learned: how to be more humble and how to respect people. I realize now I can always be more and more humble. I learnt a lot doing this movie. One of the things I learnt is how to be patient and how to be respectful. There is so much we can do to help people.

I was young when I was doing that movie and I was really enjoying it. Sometimes I think I was enjoying it too much and not being respectful at all. Ugh! I don't want to think too much about that. I don't want to dwell on negative things, but it is important to relay this because of the great lessons I learned. You have to be very aware of how you are acting, speaking and treating other people, particularly when you are well known, because people are watching you. I really want to be a great role model to young people.

I admit now that I was putting God a little bit on the side and making other things a priority in my life. I was being a professional surfer, being very successful doing a movie – becoming very well known across the world. I was not just focusing on God. That took me away from God, (although, I must admit, not too far) which is not a good thing. I was not as close to him as I am at the moment. I am not embarrassed to say all this because I learnt from everything that I went through. I learnt that God should be our main focus, our main goal.

Now I am at the best time of my life and have the best relationship with God I have ever had. I learnt many lessons and realized that God makes us walk on the right track. The movie was a great experience in life to know how to be a good child of God.

Living by faith and not by sight
After the movie was released, we went into many countries and places to tell people about my story. We saw how God does great things in peoples' lives through sharing my life's experiences as a blind man. It was the best time in my life. People would come and give their lives to Jesus because they saw how lovely God is through the movie.

The bottom line of the movie was, 'live by faith and not by sight'. This made a huge impact on people's lives. People would ask me, "What hope would folks take from this movie?" The main thing I would tell them after they saw the film was that the one thing I hope is that people don't think this movie is about me. The thing I hope is that they take home the fact that a real champion is one who follows God, who walks with Jesus and lives by faith because Jesus loves us so much and He can do great things in our lives – no matter if we are blind, or if we have any problems. He can still do great things. I hope you can understand how I can see with God's eyes and you can do the same.

The movie has been shown around 40 countries to maybe about 400,000 people, but the greatest triumph of doing the movie is not just the pleasure of surfing Pipeline and meeting great people, which was exciting. The greatest thing to me is to see how God can change people's lives through my story. In that movie, I realized God was using me as an instrument to change people's lives. That is what I appreciated the most.

Overcoming challenges

When we were filming, I was going to have a chance to go surf at Pipeline between the semi finals and the finals of the prestigious 'Pipeline Masters' contest. This is an annual event and was sponsored by the same company that sponsored me at that time. They were about to give me a chance to do a surfing presentation right before the final. I was so happy; it was a great honor for a surfer.

Not even in my most impossible dreams would I have thought that one day I could get a chance just to surf at Pipeline on my own. I was really happy and I loved that my family and friends were going to watch me because the event was going to be live on the Internet. They show the contest live globally so everyone can see it. I was excited, but nervous at the same time because I knew that everyone was going to watch me.

I was preparing and waxing my surfboard and listening to the waves crashing on the shore. It was a wonderful feeling. It was a beautiful sunny day with rainbows in the sky and there was light rain. Everything was perfect. The way the waves were breaking was perfect for me. A great wave was about to descend and the barrel that I always wanted to get was about to come. I knew I was going to have every single wave to myself because no one else was going to be out there surfing.

About one hour before my expression session, another surfer hurt himself really badly, so the people who were responsible for the contest decided to cancel my presentation for safety reasons. Another surfer also injured himself and got smashed and pounded on the rocks, so people who were in charge of the safety of the contest decided for my own safety that it would be good to cancel the expression session. They thought that could be really dangerous for me.

When I got the news that I was not able to surf anymore, I was so frustrated that I was about to cry. My dream just died. I could not believe that they cancelled it. I could not do anything to change their mind. In my mind I was asking, *Why does that have to happen to me? What did I do wrong? Why are they not letting me surf* I just wanted to be on my own, not talk with anyone. I was so sad.

About that time, I received a phone call from my parents in Brazil. Their business was not going very well so they had to shut the doors and walk away. It felt like everything bad was happening at the same time in my life. Their company was everything to me. They had had this store right in front of the ocean for about 20 years. It was where I grew up, where I made many friends, where I met many people and also where I started to have the desire to become a surfer. I would spend a lot of time listening to the waves crashing across the street in the ocean. It was a wonderful time for me, something I will never forget.

When they gave me that news, I was so frustrated that I could not handle all the bad news at the same time. To this day, I have no idea how I overcame those difficulties in my life.

I was still in Hawaii filming a movie about my life, but I kept asking, *Why is everything bad happening in my life?* I was questioning myself. In those times I was just a really sad boy; I was not that happy surfer anymore. We also had a long journey ahead to complete that movie.

I once was lost
I decided to go for a walk on my own to think about life and also to think what I could do to find happiness. While I was walking, I got lost at the village I was staying in, so I started to get nervous because I didn't know where to go. I did not have a cell phone with me to make a phone call to Bryan Jennings and also my other friends to find out where I was.
My only option was to be relaxed and wait until someone would come and find me. I was always a really smart boy. I would never get lost, so I thought there might be a reason.

It turns out, there was a reason. God wanted me to be on my own to think about life, so I realized that God wanted to talk to me. I calmed myself down and I started to think about everything that was happening at the same time in my life: not being able to surf at Pipeline right before the finals and my parents losing their business. I needed to wake up and see that all I needed was to be with God, to walk on his path and keep on the right track he had set before me.

I realized that in my whole life I had overcome challenges because I was strong and I believed in myself because I didn't want to limit myself, and going through these difficulties, it should not be any different. I still had to be strong.

When I realized that, when I finally got the revelation, I got up and started to walk and I was not lost anymore. I found my way. I found the place I needed to go to, which was the house we were staying at. It was just a great experience that I had with God. He just wanted to talk with me and show me that he's there for me, he is always with me, and he is looking after me. It was such a comforting feeling.

So I started to be happy again and to spread joy. I was enjoying being in Hawaii, which was a place that I loved to be. Surfing every day having a lot of fun, hanging out with my friends and also working hard for the movie and doing interviews every day... We were having a great time over there.

It was a time in my life that I was becoming even more famous. People were all talking about 'the blind surfer', and unfortunately I was losing my humility. I was a young boy; I just wanted to have fun, and sometimes I would hurt people's feelings without realizing it. I regret being like this. I was not acting in my normal manner. I thought that I could do everything I wanted to do. I was in the middle of the biggest surf contest of the year and the intentions were all upon myself.

As people started to hear that a blind surfer wanted to go out and get some waves at Pipeline, it blew their minds. Everyone was talking about me and I was becoming more and more famous. All of this started to go around in my mind and it changed my nature. Suddenly I started to become someone who was arrogant and not so nice to people anymore. Looking back, I am not proud of myself for that kind of behaviour. But thankfully, I realized that and saw what was happening to me in time and I could change myself back to what I was before.

I was getting some good waves in Hawaii. The team making the movie went away for a few weeks, but they were going to come back the next month so we could keep filming. Magno arrived in Hawaii a few weeks later, so he got to know Bryan Jennings and the other people working together on the movie. Spending time with Magno again was great to help me recover from my lack of humility and also to help me build up my faith in God again.

I was feeling a little bit weak and also frustrated, as I could not get a barrel at Pipeline. I was surfing pretty well, but I didn't get the barrel that I dreamt about my whole life. Magno reminded me, saying, "Derek, the journey is not only about getting the barrel at Pipeline. It's not about making yourself happy in surfing. It's not all about that, but it is about inspiring people and giving them courage and to also share your faith in God with people so it will give them hope in their heart."

Once he told me that, I thought to myself, *this is the purpose from God in my life. I have to be grateful for everything he's doing. I have to use the tools that God gave me to help people, and honestly, that is what makes me happy the whole time.*

There is nothing better than when someone comes to me and says, "Hey Derek, I love to see what you do. You really inspire me. It really encouraged me. It gives me hope when I see you accomplishing your dreams. It shows me that I can do anything." That's what I really love.

When I hear those things from people, it makes me so strong. That is the best value that I have in my life: that I can help people. That is what matters to me. Because of that, it keeps me going in trying to chase and achieve my dreams.

CHAPTER 9.

MY TIME 'DOWN UNDER'

A ustralia: a land of kangaroos, koalas, great beaches, great surf, and 'G'day mate'. I was interested in seeing this 'Land Down Under'. I mean, if it has the best surf, then I'm in. This is my life; it is what I live for. My time in Australia was one of many adventures: ups and downs, but also a time in my life of wonderful memories.

One thing that is really interesting in my adventure to Australia is that, even before surfing, my dad was telling me there are some places in the world where the waves are really good and Australia was one of them. I barely knew anything about the country. A few weeks later after my dad told me this, I dreamt I was surfing in Australia. After some time, I didn't remember this dream. I totally forgot about it and afterwards I found I was living and surfing in Australia!

The idea of moving to Australia started when I was doing some promotions for my movie, 'Beyond Sight', which was filmed in Brazil, Australia, Hawaii and California. That trip opened my eyes to this beautiful country.

When we eventually came to Australia, I was a guest speaker in a few schools and also some churches. I spoke in about ten schools, including Scots College in Sydney. We showed some of the movie and I spoke with the 'Stand Tall' team, a charity organization that runs events in schools to empower teenagers to be their best. I really enjoyed this, as it gave me the chance to relate to and inspire people up close. That is actually one of my main focuses in life. I love it! I found Sydney to be really cool and the people were really nice and extremely welcoming. I felt very comfortable and I appreciated the time I was there so much. I really felt at home.

Unstoppable

However, it was time to return to my country of birth: Brazil. A year later, after I had left Australia, the Kellogg's company contacted me. They wanted to do a campaign called 'Derek Rabelo Unstoppable'. After we signed the agreement, they traveled to Brazil to film and they also wanted to interview my parents to portray my daily life back in Brazil. People were interested to know how I overcame the challenges to surf in Pipeline in Hawaii. Yes, I must admit, this was huge.

After a few months, the company called me up to fly me to Australia to promote the campaign. My father came with me. I was actually the picture for Kellogg's breakfast cereal, promoting their *Nutri-Grain* brand. I also did some TV work for some commercial campaigns for a few channels in Australia. This was very exciting for me and exciting to be back in Australia.

I stayed in Australia for about a month for that campaign. I had a few friends over there – friends from Brazil who were living there at the time. I also had some other Australian friends I had met from the last trip. It was a great time in my life. I had such an amazing time there. I was feeling very blessed.

After the campaign finished, I then went back to America and Brazil and each day, I woke up with the idea that I would pack up and move to

Australia. I really missed the country (and particularly the surf – it is so great there). I was in California at that time so I just packed my suitcase one day and told my friend who was with me, "You know what mate, I am going to Australia. Bye bye."

That's how I did it. When I make up my mind, I really move. He was wondering what was going on. This was the last thing he was expecting. Then I called my friends in Sydney and told them I was coming to Australia to live there, hang out, get some waves, eat some tacos. In other words, to enjoy the good life.

My friends were really excited and said, "Come out to Australia, there is a bed here for you. You can stay at our house. You're more than welcome." They were good mates of mine. I definitely didn't need much persuasion! Then I moved to Sydney and I ended up staying for two years.

Many things happened while I was in Australia. I was traveling a lot and I must admit it was a great time in my life. I was surfing a lot, meeting new friends and having a great social life. This is how I began my time 'Down Under'. I will never forget it.

Before I moved to Australia I had thought it was the land of the kangaroos, great waves, beautiful beaches and nice places, and it certainly is. All of that was convincing me to go to back. Another attraction is that I would be really close to Indonesia, which is where I also wanted to go. It's not too far away, so I thought it was not a bad idea. I'm always thinking, particularly about surfing!

Standing tall

Upon reflection, there were a few reasons that made me come to Australia in 2013. The first step was that I was asked to work for Stand Tall. Being a conference for young people to soften their hearts and learn about

God, that already really interested me. We also conducted surf camps. They invited me to be a guest to Sydney. That's where God started to open the doors for me.

Jeanine Treharne, the co-founder of Stand Tall, explains, Stand Tall is designed to build hope into the lives of young people. We bring high profile Christian sports men and women to speak to young people in schools and churches and to inspire and motivate them for their lifelong journey.

"One year, Derek had a long delay in getting approval for his visa to come from Brazil to Australia. We were worried that we were getting close to our deadline and may not have Derek to speak at our event. I called in the middle of the night from Australia and spoke to someone at the Australian Embassy in Rio. I spoke to an Australian lady. They said it could be a problem allowing him in because he was blind. They were concerned that he wouldn't be independent enough. Someone in the Embassy showed that person a picture of Derek riding a huge wave in Hawaii and the lady was amazed. The visa was granted soon after. "

Since that time, my relationship with Australia started to build and became stronger and stronger. I started to make great and lasting friendships. I was so grateful for the way people welcomed me. It meant a lot to me. It made me feel like I was at home.

Nelson Powell, another friend in Sydney, remembered some fun and poignant times. "One funny incident is when we were walking down the beach. I got Derek's glasses and took his stick and it seemed he was the one leading me around. Every time people came past they assumed I was blind, and Derek would be laughing.

"We were at one of the parties after an event. There were a lot of people. And this was part of a surfing event. We were invited to go there. I remember walking Derek through the crowd. It was shoulder to shoulder and he was holding his stick and I was pulling it closer, trying to protect him. Derek took my hand off his stick. He said, 'No, when you hold my stick then I am really blind.' I was taking one of the things he could do away from him. His point of view was very interesting and made me realize that he doesn't go into anything thinking he can't do it. He thinks he can do anything. This is where he is with God. He needs to experience things."

Surfing is an amazing sport in Australia. There was a time when I thought maybe I would live in Australia forever, but I think it was a momentary thought. I do miss Australia when I'm not there. I think about it all the time. I miss the people, I miss the culture, the surfing and I miss the weather.

When I spoke in churches along the east coast and also the west coast, many people were coming to me and saying what I talked about was very good and they enjoyed hearing my story. We also showed the movie. Somehow, I became really famous in Australia because of the campaign with Kellogg's. It was on the TV all the time, even during the time of the Australian Open Tennis Championships, which everyone in Australia seems to watch. They showed that advertisement between the games for three years in a row. That was amazing.

Walking on the wrong paths
However all was not perfect. I don't like to admit it, but there was a time in Australia when I started to walk far away from God. I began to party a lot and walk with people I would not normally associate with. It was easy for me in Australia. I was single and living the high single life and I didn't have a home base. In Australia, there are many girls and they want to get to know other boys, especially guys who come from overseas. That was something that disturbed me a lot and made my life a little difficult

there. I started to stray from the path I was meant to be on. I am not embarrassed to say this because it can be an example for others.

I began to do wrong things and make wrong decisions and not be wise. I was not seeking wisdom from God. Those things led me onto the wrong path and I sincerely wanted to correct my life. I was supposed to be a witness for God. It was a very dark time in my life. I finally said to myself, *Okay Derek, that's not something that you want to do.* I didn't feel comfortable with that anymore. Eventually I stopped walking down the wrong track and I was able to get my life in order.

Indonesia

As I mentioned, when I was in Australia, I enjoyed the fact I was living very close to Indonesia, not too far from a place that I loved going to. When it was winter in Sydney, I was able to fly to Indonesia. The waves are great, it's cheap to be there, warm water, warm weather, the country smells good and there is a nice feeling of being there. It can also be really dangerous there in the ocean. The coral and the reefs under the ocean are very sharp and many people get injured. My mates would come to me and say that it looks like those surfers got out from a cage of tigers because of all those scratches and bleeding from the rocks.

There is high adrenalin for me being in Indonesia and I love it. It was a great challenge for me. Every single time I would go to the beach, it was great fun and great waves. So when it was really cold in Australia, I would go a few times to Indonesia to get away from the cold and still enjoy surfing. It was the same with Hawaii. When it was winter in Australia, I could go to Hawaii where there were great, powerful, big waves – and Hawaii is not too far from Australia and Indonesia.

The opportunity that God gave me to be on television with Kellogg's gave me an opening to share the gospel with people. Because of the exposure, many people got to know me and asked me to speak at their church or in their company. As I became well known, I was able to speak in schools, events and conferences. Through those opportunities, I shared the gospel and my personal faith.

I had some very funny occasions. One time I had to pretend I was not blind so I could rent out a jet ski in Noosa in Queensland with my friend. I put sunglasses on and left my stick at home. The people asked me to sign the papers and they believed I could ski. So I had a good time skiing – until we broke the ski. We had to bring it back. Thankfully I didn't lose my sunglasses in the ocean so I could keep pretending I was not blind. However, the owner saw me surfing and he realized I was the blind surfer. It was a bit of fun.

Dark days

Life was perfect and amazing in Australia. I could afford to pay all my bills and I was well sponsored by a few big brands. One day, I received a phone call from my boss of one of my biggest sponsors. I first received a text from her and it said, "Hey we need to have a chat with you the next morning."

I said, "Yes sure, I will do it." Then I thought something bad might be coming. They will either reduce my income or fire me.

The next morning I received the call from them and that was it. They got straight to the point and said they were going to let me go because they weren't doing so well financially. I said, "Okay, thank you for having me for the four years. I will be honest: being sponsored by you and being part of the team was great. But I'm here for you guys. Let me know about anything in the future."

They said, "Thanks for being part of our team and we wish you good luck."

I went back to my bedroom and I was fine and happy. I went down to the beach and caught up with friends. I said, "I'm not a part of the team anymore. They had to let me go."

All of my friends were disappointed and frustrated at the company. They were all asking, "How could they fire you? How could they do this? You're their best athlete, you inspire everyone."

I was thinking, *Why are they disappointed at this company? I am okay; I'm happy.*

Then a few days later, I woke up with the reality that I had lost a good sponsor. When I received the news, I was okay, but later on, everything just hit me. Then I started to feel very, very bad. I started to feel useless and used by them. I felt like I was the worst human on earth. I wanted to understand why they did this to me. I was doing such a great job for them. Everyone knew this; it wasn't just me saying that. Even my other friends on the same team were surprised.

Two months before this, one of the surfers from the same team was killed when he was shot. He was a great friend of mine. I was dealing with his death and was missing him. Then two months after this news, I was told I wasn't part of the team anymore. That was really heartbreaking. I had to look for new job opportunities, although I still had a few sponsors left.

There was another shoe company that sponsored me three months after that big surf company let me go. I called the team manager to ask him why my income was delayed for three months. I still had a contract with them. They said, "Well, I'm sorry to say, you're not a part of the team anymore. Sorry we didn't tell you earlier, but we are breaking the contract.

I said, "What are you talking about? I'm not stupid, I still work for you. My income has been delayed for three months. I was wondering what was wrong with the company. You don't even give me an explanation. You just tell me I'm not part of the team anymore. That's not the right way to kick someone out. If you want to fire anyone, at least give us notice in advance. Not just to stop and not tell us. If I hadn't called, you wouldn't have told me."

They said they were sorry, and that was it. I lost two of the three major sponsors I had. I started to think about stopping my surfing. I was not motivated at all to jump in the water. I would wake up in the morning and not feel like having breakfast, putting wax on my surfboard, or checking the waves. My mate would be texting me, asking me to surf. I would not reply immediately as I would have before. I was just totally unmotivated.

I checked my bank account, looking at my balance and I was asking myself, *How am I going to live now? What am I going to do with my life now?* I remember one day, after a month of dating my girlfriend, we went out and I had to be honest with her and I told her I couldn't keep dating her anymore because all of my sponsors left me and I had no money. Then I was crying at the dining table in the middle of the restaurant. She came and hugged me and she said, "I want to be with you, no matter what because I love who you are and I love everything you are doing for God, so I will go on that journey with you."

So that gave me strength and it made me remember that I never wanted to be a surfer because of money. I never wanted to start to surf because I wanted to be a professional surfer. But it was my desire. I wanted to accomplish my dreams, so I could not let those facts and disappointments drive me away.

But God...

I moved to Perth and had a great time. It was there that I met my beautiful wife, Madeline, who was the girlfriend that I have just been talking about. So that has become a special place for me. My life suddenly changed. I definitely made the right decision when I was in California to move to Australia!

Adam Hansen, a friend from Perth, commented: "We spent a lot of time together and I helped train him, as I am a personal trainer. We did a lot of balance work and coordination balance training using a slack line – like a width of a seat belt and you tie it like tightrope walking. He made it with eight steps. He is very fit and very well coordinated.

"We went surfing on the weekends. We drove up to different locations. One time we drove to a beach an hour's drive north of Perth. We went four wheel driving and we were bogged for four hours. We also did local trips around town."

Pastor Margaret Court, the former world champion tennis player, remembered Derek well. "I met Derek Rabelo when he came to speak at our city-wide youth group. I was impacted by his story, his humility and his strength of character and his obvious trust in and love for God.

"Derek was a warm and friendly personality. Nothing seemed to offend or upset him and he certainly carried an air about him that nothing was impossible for him and that he hadn't let his lack of natural vision define what he could or couldn't do.

"Derek attended our Victory Life International Bible Training School for a few months and was an inspiration to the international and local students and would challenge and encourage them to follow their dreams and have a vision for their future. He was truly an inspiration to others who thought they had some type of handicap or disability.

"I know Derek will be such an inspiration to many young people in the world."

So I had started to get back to my surfing and my friend Adam was a great influence, I became the same person I was before, with or without the sponsors. I started to think that I could be happy with whatever the future would hold for me. This was a big breakthrough. My thinking had changed and it changed my perspective on life.

I admit that it was a tough time in my life that I had to go through. I had some dark times and thoughts, but I praise God that I could overcome all of this. Sometimes challenges are not only the size of the wave you ride, the amount of white water that holds you under the ocean, the physical injuries you get. It's not only those, but all those ups and downs we have to go through that can shake our emotional state. This can be really hard to get over, but I'm glad that I made it. I made it because right in the bottom of my heart, I always kept the flame of my desires alive – even thought it was very little and almost burnt out – but I kept it.

It was not too long after that the wound of losing my sponsors was healed and closed. I was not even thinking about that incident anymore. Another big company that was sponsoring me emailed me. I thought that was good, that they were calling me to give me an upgrade on my income, as they do every year when they renew the contract. When I read the email, they said unfortunately they were not going to renew the contract because they were changing their staff and their athletes and they had changed to a different ideology in their company. Even though this was a huge financial loss for me, I was already thinking that nothing was going to sway me and I kept to that. Immediately, I replied politely, thanking them for having me.

Life kept going and I was even happier. Ninety percent of my income was gone, but I was happy. I had joy in my life, I had friends, a beautiful family and God was with me and He's bigger than any sponsor or income I would have, so I knew I didn't need anything else. It was wonderful to see how that news didn't hit me at all. My whole attitude changed – I felt so free, and freedom is what God wants us to have.

CHAPTER 10.

LOVE IS IN THE AIR

I met the most beautiful girl in the world in Perth Western Australia. That event changed my life completely. I was so blessed. To have a woman by your side is just the most wonderful thing.

At the time, I was in Sydney and Jeanine Treharne from *Stand Tall* was organizing a trip to go to Western Australia to go to churches and schools for speaking engagements. I was so excited to go there, as the waves were good as well. (Priorities are very important). I was going with my friend Luis.

Prior to going to WA I had been in the time of my life where I didn't want to get married. I was quite content and happy being single. Life was good. I had a great social life, great waves and I was living the dream. However, one day I felt I was tired of all that socializing. I wanted to stop going out to parties and doing all the social things I had been used to. I realized it wasn't satisfying me. I thought to myself, *I just want to focus on my surfing and focus on God.* Then two months later I met Madeline, the girl of my dreams.

Madeline

When I arrived in WA, I felt so comfortable there. We landed quite late at night, then we went to the place I was to stay at. The next morning, I had been invited to speak at a church service for a church called C3. After I spoke, I greeted all the people who came up to me and introduced themselves. It was a great morning and I was getting to know more people, which made me feel a bit more settled.

So in Perth I had a number of speaking engagements, which I was pleased about. I loved being in Perth and I was beginning to feel that something different was going to happen while I was there, something wonderful. It was quite strange. It was my intuition kicking in.

One night I was speaking at Victory Life Centre, the church pastured by a former tennis great. This ended up being the church where my future wife, Maddy, worshiped. Maybe this was the reason I was feeling that something good was going to happen… I didn't shave my beard; I just chilled, wearing my shorts and tee shirt. I didn't brush my hair – not even my teeth! I was not planning to meet anyone – not any girl, I mean.

I met Margaret Court as she was leading the service that night. Then I spoke and shared some good things about my life and my experiences with God. After I finished, I sat in the front row with my friend Luis. Then the band started to play and the service had concluded and people were greeting each other. While I was sitting in the front row a girl suddenly danced in front of the church with some friends.

She tripped over my foot as she was dancing. Suddenly I felt something poking my foot and I wondered what was going on. I twisted to my side and there was the girl. She was feeling so sorry and embarrassed, but I thought she was so cute. I knew she was beautiful. I told her not to worry; it was cool. Then she took advantage of the moment and asked if she could have a picture taken with me. I obviously said yes and took the advantage back and hugged her. I realized she had lovely long hair. That was it for the moment. I was told later she was impressed with my kindness. I also heard that she had said to Marika, Margaret Court's daughter, that she thought I was very sweet. This is how Maddy and I connected. It was quite amazing and funny.

Maddy says, "I felt Derek's story was so inspiring. I saw some videos and I thought the way he was surfing was impossible, as he is blind. I never thought I would meet him. It was more that he inspired me, so I wanted to meet this guy. He was amazing. There was nothing romantic for me at this stage. I was worshiping God, jumping and dancing and accidentally jumped on his foot. I felt so bad. He was the guest speaker and blind. How could I have done that? I turned around and he was very nice about the incident. I then asked for a photo and he touched my hair. He told me later that when he touched my hair he told his friend Luis, 'I think I am going to marry this woman.'"

Luis and I then went to dinner with the pastors of the church. We were all chatting about life and just enjoying each other's company, then the subject of the German girl, Maddy, came up and they kept talking about her. I didn't fully understand what they were saying, but they said she was beautiful. I said, "Yes she's beautiful, she has nice long hair."

The next morning when I woke up, I had a call from Jeanine Treharne asking how the talks were going. I said that they were amazing and straight away she changed the subject and said, "Derek, there is a German girl there and she thinks you are gorgeous."

Then I said, "What a coincidence. I think she is gorgeous too."

I told Jeanine to ask the girl to come to the Christian Surfers night where I was speaking again. Then Jeanine said, "Yes I will do it." She sounded really excited. She was always thrilled to see me with someone who was really nice. She was definitely trying to get Maddy and I together. What a great friend.

Then I received a text from Marika saying the girl was coming to the Christian Surfers talk and her name was Madeline. I thought, *What a long name.* Then Marika said straight away, "You can call her Maddy." Oh what a relief. Mind you, I really love the name Madeline, but Maddy is so much easier.

So all that day I was thinking about the German girl with the long hair and the long name, but after a few hours, I had forgotten her name. Then Luis and I went to the Christian Surfers meeting and we were talking about this girl and I had no idea of her name. I thought to myself, *if she comes over to me I wouldn't know if it was the right girl. What do I do?* Then Luis and I came up with a plan. If anyone came to me, Luis would introduce himself and ask the girl's name. So the girl with the longest name would be her. What an ingenious plan we set up… This was brilliant!

Finally, she arrived and she said her name was Madeline. Then we talked a bit and I was already in love with her – definitely in love. I just knew it. Then the meeting started and I was speaking for a while. The organizers opened up the event for people to ask me questions. Maddy asked 3,500 questions. Well, it seemed like that many. I was trying to answer all these questions as best I could.

When the meeting was over, I was hanging around chatting to people. Maddy and I were trying to communicate with each other, but everyone wanted to talk to me. Maddy didn't give anyone a chance. It was a little difficult to have this time with her, so I pretended I needed to go to the restroom and I asked her if she would show me where this was. It was inside the house and my plan was to go inside where it was quieter and have some special time with her. So as we were talking and spending time together and I was getting to know her, I was already thinking, *I only have five days left here in Perth – five days to work this out. I have to make sure this girl is mine. How do I do this?*

A cunning plan

So I asked Maddy out to dinner. She said, "I have a really busy schedule, but on Wednesday we could go out after I finish my shift at 9 p.m. I thought to myself, *Wednesday is too far away; why not tomorrow night?* So I asked her.

She said, "Tomorrow night I dance salsa. I do this every Tuesday."

I thought, *I hate dancing, it's so boring and this girl dances salsa.* So I said, "That's wonderful. My dream is to dance salsa I really want to do this."

She said, "Oh great, I'll teach you tomorrow." I'm really not that devious, but a guy has to do what he has to do. Right?

I thought, *What am I doing? I hate salsa.* But I had to do this to spend more time with Maddy, so… Then the next night we went dancing and we talked a lot and got to know each other more. I am a terrible dancer, but I wanted to see if she could dance with her eyes closed so I could lead her, and she did. The night was really nice and I was even more in love with her, but I was not too sure about how she felt.

I had been feeling a bit anxious about meeting Maddy again. The next night, my friend drove me to where we had organized to meet. It was a little park in front of the bay on the water. She had her guitar and was singing and we were talking. We were talking about life and just getting to know each other a little more.

After a while, I asked if I could touch her face with my hands and she said yes. After that I gave her a kiss. She was not very happy, as she wasn't expecting me to do that. Then she told me she was so confused, but we still kept talking and I was hugging her because she was cold.

That was the night. I got an Uber back to where I was staying and when I got home, I told Luis that we kissed. He was excited, but I said, "I don't know if she was happy about this, but I did kiss her and I don't regret it – it is done. Let's see what will happen now."

I was a bit anxious the next day. At the same time, I was having a very busy schedule in Perth. Every day, I would have to speak in at least one school. There was definitely a lot going on. I woke up the next day and Luis and I were driving to the school where I had a speaking engagement. Then I had a text from Maddy saying, "Good morning, I heard you were coming to the school where I help out making breakfast. I was wondering if you would like me to make you some toast and jam?"

Then I said to Luis, "I don't think she would offer to make me toast and jam if she wasn't interested in me." So, another step forward?

We went to the school and that was my day. I ate the toast, but we didn't see each other for the rest of the time. The next day, I was only thinking about her. Then there was a youth night at Victory Life Centre where I was speaking again. Maddy was helping out and setting up food, then she came up to me and gave me a bunch of carrots. I said, "What are you thinking? Are carrots good for my sight?"

She said, "No, I just want to give you something."

We were hanging out and dancing together. Everyone in the church was talking about Maddy and I. Then in front of everyone, I kissed her hand. I had to leave Perth and go down to Margaret River, which is three hours from Perth. All I could think about was Maddy – not even the waves. I was not even thinking about my speech. My heart was going crazy about her, but I knew that in a few days, I would be leaving Australia for three months. I was thinking, *How would it work if I was dating that girl? She is studying and working. How would things happen?"*

We were texting back and forth while I was in Margaret River, then we started to talk on the phone every night. We would spend three hours on the phone just talking to each other. I was just so in love with her and getting to know her. She was planning to come down to Margaret River on the following weekend. I was so thrilled about that and I promised her I would teach her to surf.

When Maddy arrived, we spent the whole weekend together. She stayed at someone else's home. I took the plunge and asked her if she wanted to be my girlfriend and she said yes. I immediately told my mother, not my father, at this stage and Maddy told her parents and everyone was so pleased for both of us.

The last two days of my stay in Australia, I went back to Perth. Maddy and I were so in love. I had to pack my things, get a flight back to Sydney, then fly back to Brazil. I was to spend two months there, before going to Indonesia. On my last day in Perth, I was late going to the airport – on purpose. I really did want to miss my flight. I wanted to spend another day with Maddy. When the airline said I couldn't get on my flight because I was late, I pretended to be sad. They told me they could put me on a flight the next day and I told them that was awesome. Then Maddy drove me back to where I was staying and the next morning we had breakfast together, with her homemade jam on toast and a nice tea. How kind she was. I thought how very well I had organized this!

Then Maddy drove me back to the airport and we both had tears in our eyes. We hated leaving each other. After that, we would speak on the phone for three to four hours. In the meantime, I was trying to persuade her to come to Indonesia. She didn't want to come and I was trying to understand why. She didn't want to go because she had a very tight schedule and the flights were very expensive at the time. I offered to buy her ticket, but she didn't want to accept that. I ended up buying her a ticket and said, "You have to come. I have your ticket." Then she came to Bali which was great because my father was there and he had a chance to meet my beautiful girl.

When I went to pick Maddy up from the airport, I was so excited, but I must admit I had butterflies as I hadn't seen her for about 45 days. I really missed her. If she hadn't come to Indonesia, we would have been apart for three months. We had a wonderful time in Indonesia. Maddy got to know my father and we became even closer as a couple. She was also able to watch me surfing.

Falling in love

Maddy was sleeping in a bedroom, my father in the other bedroom and I was sleeping in the lounge-room. Each night when she went to the bathroom, she would pass by me and stop and give me a kiss. One night when she gave me a kiss, she put her hand near me and I grabbed her ring finger and said, "I love you." I was wondering why I had grabbed that finger. It was such a romantic time. Being in love is so beautiful.

The time passed too quickly and she had to go back to Australia. I stayed in Indonesia surfing with my father and it was so good spending time together. After Indonesia, I flew back to Sydney and was thinking about going over to Perth to spend time with Maddy. Jeanine and I were talking continuously. She came to me and said, "Derek, you've got to propose to her. Ask her to marry you. See if she is the one God has for you." But I had only known her for two months.

I didn't have a ring at that time and I was still in Sydney for another week. I was thinking about what Jeanine had said and was praying about this, also talking to my mother and grandmother, as I respect them very much. I wanted to propose to Maddy, but they thought it was a crazy idea, as I hadn't known her for very long.

On the day I was preparing to move to Perth with all my belongings, Jeanine came to me and said, "Here is a brand new ring. If you like it take it and propose to her." I thanked her very much. I was praying to God so much and asking for His wisdom. Then I moved to Perth for a new life, new journey, new friends, but no waves! What was I thinking? No waves! When I arrived there, it was such a challenge for me, as Maddy had to travel for the first few weekends and she was very busy during the week. But she helped me so much. She bought me many things for my new room. She was being such an amazing girlfriend, even though she had such a busy schedule.

While studying in the morning and working in the afternoons and evenings, she would still make the time to spend with me. On the weekends, when she could spend time with me, she was committed to go to a camp. I was really upset about that as I didn't see her side at all. I was in Perth on my own and didn't know anyone. I was just so frustrated, but I had to go through that. However, I did use that time to talk to God and get His wisdom of what to do with my life, so that was a good thing.

After a few weeks of returning to Perth, Maddy's birthday arrived. This was the first birthday we had spent together. I bought her some lovely perfume and flowers and we had a special time together and also with her friends, but I was still not sure if she even liked me, even though she said she loved me.

Suddenly, a few days after her birthday, I knew she would have the whole day off, as it was a holiday. On the day before, she told me she didn't want to see me that day. I felt very sad. I said, "You have such a busy schedule, on your day off you don't want to see me?" She also said not to call her. I just respected that, even though I was very disappointed. I didn't understand it. I didn't see her at all during that day. Well, at dinnertime she called me and I was so excited. She sounded happy and said, "Hey, I want to cook you dinner. I'll tell you something when you're here." Of course I wondered what that would be.

The 'one'

I went to her house and she looked beautiful. She made me an amazing dinner, with a lovely dessert. She told me the reason she wanted to be on her own is that she wanted to talk to God to ask Him if I was the one. God spoke clearly and said I was the one and she was to keep dating me.

Maddy said, "Many non-Christians and even Christians were saying to me, 'Are you sure about this?' All of them doubted the validity of this relationship. Many people said, 'It's going to be so hard. You want to have children and he is blind. It won't be easy.'

"God showed me when you arrived tonight that you were the one. I had a different feeling when I opened the door and saw you. A feeling of love and peace."

Maddy told me this when we were having dinner. I said, "I'm so pleased you love me and I'm totally committed to this relationship." We had a great time together and I had so much peace. I remember I dreamt one day I was getting some gold rings for Maddy. A few days after I dreamt that Jeanine was telling me that I should not waste time; I should propose, as she was the girl for me.

I told my mother and grandmother what I was going to do and they were praying. I told my father as well, he was a bit concerned, but I made the decision to propose to her. I got the ring Jeanine gave me and took Maddy out to dinner. I chose a really nice restaurant. We had a lovely dinner, but I was so nervous, so I didn't propose to her! I just couldn't do it. I went back home and was annoyed with myself. *How could I have missed such a great opportunity?'* I thought to myself.

Then God spoke to me and told me to go and buy a ring for Maddy. I told her best friend and asked her to help me choose a ring, as she knew Maddy's taste. She went to the mall with me and we checked out a few jewelry stores. She showed me some rings and I did choose one – the one

I thought would be the best for my beautiful woman – and I took the ring home. It was a stunning vintage ring, with nice diamonds on the top.

The 'question'

Then a few days later, I asked her out for dinner again. I wanted to do something on the beach, but it was winter and far too cold, so I took her to a nice revolving restaurant in Perth. She wasn't aware of what I was planning. It was a very rainy day unfortunately, but I was determined it would be fantastic – a great day in my life. Before we arrived, someone had organized a bouquet of beautiful flowers to be set on the table.

I was hoping and praying this time around, it would be successful. When we arrived at the restaurant, I thought, *This dinner will be really expensive.* I decided I would propose before the dinner because if she said no, we could leave. I am always thinking! However, I had second thoughts about this strategy, so we instead ordered our meals. I told her to close her eyes, then I said to her, "Will you marry me?"

She said, "Will you wear a bowtie to the wedding?"

I thought this was a strange question to ask, so I asked the question again, "Will you marry me?"

She said yes, so I put the engagement ring on her finger and she gave me a kiss.

Then she told me, "You realize this is forever?"

I said, "Yes, I know." I was so relieved and excited. I just loved the romance at the time. I really think I am a romantic at heart! Then we had dessert and went back to the place we were staying. Maddy sent text messages to her family and friends. We were so excited and thankful that God had brought us together.

The next day at church, we told Marika we were engaged and she was so happy and told everyone in the church and they all wanted to see the ring. The whole church was ablaze with the excitement of an engagement, then a wedding. So finally, I was engaged to Maddy! All we could talk about was the wedding and how and where we wanted it, which was on a beach at sunset.

But at the same time, I was trying to live my life in Perth doing what I was meant to do. This was extremely difficult because there were not many waves. However, not everything was rosy. When I was living in Perth, I was far from everything. I would have to get the bus and train wherever I wanted to go. I was becoming a little depressed because of this. Maddy realized I was not happy. She had a talk to me and I said that living here was not so good for me. It was very far from everything and to be engaged – all this was a huge challenge for me. I did not know how to handle all this. I was also living with people I didn't really know. Sometimes I would sleep 15-18 hours a day because I wasn't motivated to do anything.

This should have been a very happy time in my life, having just becoming engaged, but I was very depressed. Maybe I was just wondering to myself, *Am I doing the right thing?* I think that if I had more to do in Perth, life would have been a little easier, but what can you do? There are a number of varying seasons in your life and you just have to flow with them.

I started Bible College at Victory Life Centre in Perth, but life was still very challenging. I had never felt this way before. I actually started to hate Perth. Those few months when I was there were very tough. I was about to get married and live in a place that I hated! The devil tried to say to me, "Well, what has this girl done to you? You're not enjoying life, you are living in a city you don't like. You're not happy and you're not surfing and you don't have many friends. Why don't you go back to Sydney where you have many friends, you can surf and go to parties?"

All the time, I was trying to stay strong and close to God. Every time I would bow before him, I would ask for wisdom and strength. A few months later, I planned to go on a speaking tour to New Zealand. Maddy drove me to the airport. I was going with Rosemaree Knight, who had organized and planned all the engagements for me. I was interested as to how God would work that trip. I had only one speaking engagement booked, but I still booked my flight knowing God would open all the right doors for me. The time to go to NZ was getting closer and God just opened up many opportunities to speak: schools, churches and movie showings. I ended up speaking to about 5,000 people in NZ. I got some good waves and formed some great new friendships. I was also able to see a great friend who I hadn't seen for a long time. However, it was difficult, as I was away from Maddy.

When I was in NZ, I sent Maddy some beautiful flowers. I wanted her to feel so loved. It was the first time I had been away from her since we were engaged. We were so in love and talked on the phone each day. From the first day I met Maddy, I would send her flowers every few weeks, even if I was away. That's how much I loved her.

Flying back from NZ, I did a stopover in Sydney and Maddy came to meet me. She got to know my good friends there. Everyone was like family to me. I didn't have my real family in Australia and I wanted to make sure everyone met Maddy. We spent a whole week in Sydney together.

Finally, I went back to Perth. I was going to move away to another home near the ocean where I could do everything: walk to the beach, the gym, the grocery store, places where I didn't need to be driven to. Then I started to enjoy Perth. That was a relief. I met some new friends in the area I had moved to and I became a new Derek. Not depressed or unmotivated, I was happy once again.

Some little changes in our lives can make all the difference. Moving to another area changed me completely. It made a huge difference to me. I met a guy called Adam Hansen, who worked at the gym, which was next door to where I lived. Maddy initially took me and asked Adam to show me around. He was very confused at first. Maddy left me and he didn't know what to do with me. I said to him, "Just show me where the machine is." He didn't seem very friendly, but he was very polite. Then after a short time, we became great friends. We worked out, surfed, went on road trips and just hung out together. so he complimented my life a little more in Perth. I had someone to share life with.

I was finally happy in Perth. I was enjoying being engaged to my fiancée and preparing for the wedding. Then Maddy and I planned to go to Germany before the wedding so I could meet her parents and family. She had not met my family, other than my father in Bali, so I felt it was only fair that I go to Germany and meet her parents and family members so they could get to know me.

Meeting Maddy's family

Maddy explains, "I had told my mother I had met a guy in the church and he was blind. She had mixed feelings about this. I told her that he surfs and there was a move about him, so she Googled him and got to know more about him. She was very surprised and inspired by what he had accomplished and how he lived his life. My mother thought a lot about our engagement and often couldn't sleep at night. She thought a lot about our relationship and felt deep down that it was right and would work. She had a good feeling about it. Everything she read was positive and inspiring.

"Previously Derek had asked my mother and father if he could marry me, but this was after the engagement, so we flew to Germany and had a stopover in Hong Kong. We had a little holiday there and took some time to discover the mysteries and diversity of that country."

After a great time we then went on to Germany. When we arrived there, it was winter and super cold, as you can imagine. It was down to minus degrees. Not what I was used to! Maddy had promised me that Christmas would be a wonderful time with snow. When we arrived in Germany, it was below zero, but there was no sign of snow. Maddy's mother picked us up at the train station. The interesting thing was that her mother had not seen Maddy for over a year, but she went straight to me and hugged me instead of her daughter. I just felt so accepted and welcomed and loved. It was so great to feel that from my future mother-in-law.

We went straight to Maddy's house. I remember it was such a cold country. The food was interesting: there was only sausages, potatoes and cabbage. Not quite what I was used to! I hadn't met her father at that stage. Later, Maddy went out with her mother and I stayed at home. I was in the living room and her father came in, speaking no English, so I had no idea what he was talking about. *This is going to be interesting,* I said to myself. I pretended I understood him. I said, "Great to meet you. Excited to have you at our wedding. I love your daughter." He was very nice so I felt welcomed by the family.

"At times, it was really hard while they were in Germany," Maddy's mother said. "Maddy was working, I couldn't speak English and I couldn't even make signs because Derek couldn't see. Maddy and Derek then used Google translator to cover the communication difficulties.

"At Christmas one time, Maddy was at work and it started to snow, so I took Derek out to show him the snow. I gave him some chores to do and it was fun watching him work. He enjoyed doing this."

"My father offered Derek a black beer," Maddy explained. "Dad had a crate of beer and Derek, out of politeness, drank it, but he hated it. This was not what he was used to. My father went to the bathroom and Derek threw the beer out. Then dad offered him another. He always offers Derek this black beer when he sees him, but Derek does not have the heart to say that he doesn't like it.

"Then we went ice skating, but Derek could not skate. We went on what we thought was a normal ice skating day – but it wasn't! There were a lot of students there and they all laughed at the way Derek was trying to skate. I felt a bit sorry for him. but he didn't seem to mind."

Maddy's mother said, "Because Maddy was working a lot, Derek was home and he was sometimes bored. I just didn't know what to do because of the language barrier and the blindness."

"Derek was preparing to ride some big waves, so he had to train a lot and we had to go to the gym," Maddy explained. "Someone had to go with him to show him the machines. We walked to the gym and it was really cold. At the gym, Derek would ask someone to show him how to train for his shoulders, but instead they would find something for his arms. Unfortunately they always found the wrong machines for him."

I stayed in Germany for a few weeks and we ended up having a great Christmas and New Year with Maddy and her family. Then I had to leave Maddy alone again in Germany, as I had to go to Hawaii for some work and to surf. I was gone for three weeks, and while I love Hawaii, it was very difficult being away from Maddy. I was counting the days to be reunited with her. Normally I don't want to leave Hawaii. That must have been true love!

CHAPTER 11.

THE WEDDING OF THE YEAR...

Ever since we became engaged, Maddy and I would talk about the wedding constantly – where it would be, when and who we would invite. We certainly we had many friends. Everything we had to choose and think about caused us to have little arguments, which I think was probably normal. I was sure it was normal!

At first my grandmother Cleuza, who I love and respect so much, called me to talk about the wedding and to encourage me to do what my heart and God were telling me to do. She was concerned about me. Then she asked me what I wanted to do and I said that I love Maddy and I wanted to marry her, but she was concerned it was too soon. Then my grandmother was praying with me and telling me she got married when she was 15 years-old. She explained to me that the time is not what matters – what mattered was that God was preparing this woman for me and I had to be wise. So I got a lot of encouragement from her. The reason I wanted to talk to my grandmother was because I have a lot of respect for her and we have a good relationship. She is a wonderful woman.

THE WEDDING OF THE YEAR...

Decisions decisions...
So I knew what was in my heart. The first decision we made together was that we wanted to get married at the beach at sunset. This was non-negotiable. We loved the idea of the ceremony at the beach. We both agreed that we would get married at Margaret River, where we officially became a couple. Also it is a world-renowned surf break, so there was a good meaning about that place. Margaret River is a beautiful place.

So the first thing we did was to make a list of people to invite. We completed this and so our guest list was perfect. We had all the people we wanted to come, or so we thought. In the first few weeks after we got engaged, planning the wedding became a real challenge and we had a number of disagreements. Then unfortunately, more arguments started to happen in our relationship. I think God was starting to challenge us to see if we really loved each other. Oh well, they say true love doesn't always run smooth!

The problem was that Maddy only wanted to think about the wedding and I only wanted to think about the honeymoon. She wanted the best wedding and I wanted the best honeymoon. The first resolution was to decide a date for the wedding, which was going to be February 23rd 2017. This was ten months after we met. We chose that date because it would suit both Maddy's and my parents. Our first requirement was to choose a date for both families, as they would have to come a long way. Then I went to a travel agency with Maddy and after many hours of indecisions and thinking and talking and not agreeing on things, Maddy saw some pictures of the Maldives then we made a decision together to spend our honeymoon in the Maldives and also in Thailand. So we had two weeks for our honeymoon. Subsequently, this was sorted out and I was happy and Maddy was also. Phew, another good resolution was made.

But then the big fight started. I booked this honeymoon, which I thought was a gift from God. We invested a lot of money into this, but there was not much left for the wedding. Now the problems started! Then Maddy started to be worried and we had a huge fight because of that honeymoon. We almost cancelled it. We thought that Maddy should go back to Germany with her parents and I go back to Brazil so we could work and save money for the wedding, but we quickly realized that was a stupid idea. We prayed and God gave us wisdom and strength, so we both stayed in Australia and God provided everything for us. Why did we doubt that he would?

But we didn't have a great deal of time to prepare for a wedding. We finally chose the place for the ceremony. We got this beautiful place at Margaret River where we could get married on the beach and have the reception on a deck, just the way we dreamed. I must say it was very difficult at first to make the choice about this venue as it was very expensive. However, we still booked the place we really wanted and relied on God.

God was giving all these opportunities to us and we couldn't fully understand how great God works. It was so wonderful. We both felt so blessed. Why do we doubt at times? The beach where the reception was was almost like a little bay. It was called Gnarabup Beach. It had one little jetty on the right hand side and beautiful mountains on the other side.

A stressful time

At this stage, we were getting very excited about the wedding, but the time leading up to the wedding was the hardest on our relationship. Every single decision was difficult. We both had our own opinions and we wanted to stick to these, each of us wanting our own way. When we started to list the guests for the wedding, the biggest issue we had was that my parents didn't have enough money to come all the way from Brazil. Flights were so expensive. We didn't know what to do. So the time was moving on and we had signed up an agreement for the wedding reception. We gave the owners the list of guests. We had people from ten countries to the wedding. Ten different nationalities – that was amazing and so exciting.

We finally finished the list and with a miracle from God, we could pay the deposit. We were trying to get everything ready for the wedding, but we still had the issue of my parents. Then Maddy came to me and said, "Derek, we cannot have the wedding without your parents, so we either pay for the flight or we don't get married now." We both agreed we should book their tickets. I had no idea where money was coming from, but God was providing all the way. That was one more lesson I learnt from God: he had everything prepared for our wedding. He was in control of everything.

While we were starting to prepare for the wedding, my mother heard from God. He was telling her that he was going to give Maddy the wedding of her dreams. I shouldn't worry about anything; he was preparing the wedding for us. When we started to prepare for the big event, my mother was praying all the time for us that we would not fall into temptation, as our relationship was from God. The enemy really wanted to come into our lives and make us fall and fight and become angry with each other. She was always praying and trying to help us.

Finally, a couple of months before the wedding, we were able to book my parents' tickets, so that took a lot of stress off us. We knew we would have both sets of parents there with us on this wonderful and special occasion. My grandmother was planning to come as well, but when the wedding date was getting closer, for some reason she felt like she would not be able to come. She was really upset she had to make that decision, but her husband was very sick and she couldn't leave him alone. So she called me saying, "Derek I'm very sorry and upset that I'll be missing the wedding. It is really difficult for me, but I can't leave him on his own. You know what he is going through in his health situation." I was really upset to hear this news. That was really frustrating for me because a big member of my family was not going to be there.

For a short while I was a little disappointed and anxious because I wanted to have my grandmother in attendance, but afterwards, I felt bad having those thoughts. I thought I was being selfish. I didn't tell her what I was feeling but I did feel bad about being disappointed and anxious. We kept moving ahead with out wedding plans. The day was getting closer. We already had the guest list finalized, which had been given to the people at the venue. But we did meet some new people and became really good friends with them. However we couldn't invite them to the wedding because it would be an extra cost and we had exhausted our budget. But after a lot of talk with Maddy, we decided to invite them because they were such good friends to us. We were thankful we made that decision because today they mean a lot to us.

So February 23 was coming up quickly. A few weeks before, we started to receive people from overseas. From all around the world, they started to arrive in Australia. Maddy's family and friends, my family and friends - having all those people arriving at the same time was amazing and really exciting. But at the same time it was very stressful, especially for Maddy. She had to finish preparing for the wedding and also give attention to her family, friends and my family and friends. Maddy also had to work every day, but we were so grateful that everyone could come and we wished we could give each one of them more attention.

Unfortunately, fights between Maddy and I kept happening as the wedding was getting closer and we were worried. However, we both agreed we were not being wise in a lot of our decision-making and attitudes and there was a lot of stress on us. Fortunately, we were able to realize this and deal with it.

A 'blessed' dress
Since we had been engaged, Maddy was looking for wedding dresses, trying to find the perfect one. She had actually been looking for a wedding dress from when we first met. We would be talking on the phone and at the same she was looking at wedding dresses online. Sometimes when we were talking, she would get quiet and I would wonder why she wasn't talking. She then told me about that little scenario when we got engaged. She started to go with her bridesmaids and friends to look for dresses. I was not to know anything about the dress. She was always spending time with her friends talking about it – nothing else. Every Friday evening, they would have meetings to talk about the dress. I found this annoying because I wanted to spend that time with her. Then Maddy told me she was going to order a dress on a Chinese website because it was really cheap. I jumped up and down and told her, "You're not going to marry me with a dress made in China and you don't even know if it will fit. I don't agree with that."

She said, "Derek, we can't afford anything more expensive. It only cost a few hundred dollars."

I said, "Don't worry, God will provide a dress. Keep looking and he will provide the money."

One day we were at church and I met a lady who is a wedding dress designer of the highest quality dresses. Her dresses are in the price range around $5,000 to $7,000. She is really good in what she does. She said, "Hi Derek, I hear you're getting married."

I said, "Yes very soon."

"Does your fiancé have a wedding dress?" she asked.

"She's looking for a dress," I said.

Then the designer said, "I am a wedding dress designer. Tell your fiancé to come to my store. I have many options for her to choose from."

I thought, *She may think we are rich.*

Then I told Maddy, "Honey, I met this lady and she designs wedding dresses. You should go and see them."

She said, "I'm not going to go there. It's so expensive."

I did agree with her, but encouraged her to go. Then she listened to me and went to see her, and then God started to work again. So the dress designer wanted to bless us with a dress that cost $5,000. She gave Maddy the dress. The only thing Maddy had to pay for were the adjustments that cost about $200 and that was it. What a miracle!

It was just one more lesson how God works in our life and how we should always rely on him. We are so limited in our faith and thinking and in the meantime we have a great God who loves us, and if we seek his kingdom first, everything else will be added. All we need is to walk with God, worship him and be grateful for everything he does and that happens in our lives.

Another miracle

The wedding was still getting closer. Two days before the wedding, we were down south in Margaret River. We had both of our families and friends in this tiny little town. It was great having everyone around and hanging out with everyone, but there was one thing missing from the wedding, which was a car to bring Maddy to the ceremony. We were not to worry about that as we could ask anyone to drive her, but Maddy always dreamt about having one of those fancy, old-fashioned cars to bring her, but once again that was out of our price range. We would have to get someone to drive her to the ceremony.

Two days before the wedding, we were having lunch with some of our friends and suddenly Maddy looked outside. She called out excitedly, "Honey, honey."

I said, "What's going on?"

She said, "Parked here is a beautiful, amazing antique car that people use in movies for weddings. It's the most beautiful car ever."

I replied, "Oh cool. If it's that old it may not work." The driver had said to Maddy that he likes to take people for a drive.

Maddy explained, "I asked him if he wants to drive me to the wedding and the driver said that yes, he also does that. I said, 'Cool, but I don't have the money.' Then he told me that would only charge $200 to drive me to the wedding and drive us to our hotel after.

"I explained that it would be amazing, but we couldn't spend any more money. We couldn't afford it. We prayed to God that if he wanted us to have that car, that he would provide."

Maddy agreed. She wanted to have that car so badly and I really wanted her dream to be fulfilled.

We prayed about it and we both agreed we could not spend the money. A few hours later, her friend, one of her bridesmaids, offered to pay for the car as a wedding gift. We were so grateful to her and to God. Our mind was just blown away. How much can God bless us? How great is God?

We were able to get the car, which was so wonderful, particularly for Maddy. One day before the wedding, Maddy and I were trying to agree on something small and we ended up having the worst fight of our lives. I was trying to understand why all of the fighting was happening. I knew I could be a better man and she knew she could be a better woman. Why was God letting this happen? If we were already fighting that bad, why get married? Bad thoughts were coming into my mind and I was thinking about giving up on our marriage. Yes, we had fights, but we never wanted to give up on our marriage.

Every day before the wedding, it was very cloudy and drizzling. The forecast for the wedding didn't look good – it was going to be overcast, but I was not worrying too much, instead leaving it up to God. Maddy too was praying a lot for good weather. When we woke up on the wedding day, the sky and ocean were beautiful. it was amazing. I kept going outside and saying, "Oh God, how great you are." He was preparing every detail as he always does.

The night before the wedding I had a great and special time having dinner with my groomsmen: Nelson, Ted, Scott and Luis and my best man was my father. I was going to have Bryan Jennings as my best man, but because of some health issues with his wife, he could not attend the wedding. However, it was wonderful having my father in my wedding party. I could barely sleep, I was so nervous. I was praying to God, asking for directions for the big day before going to sleep. I was also talking with my mum, dad and good friends.

The day

On the wedding day I just wanted to relax. I wanted to surf with my wedding party – just the boys – at my favorite surfing break at Margaret River. We had a great surf. I was so blessed the waves were amazing. I had so much fun, getting waves and sharing with the guys. This was a really nice way to begin the wedding day.

After that I had breakfast with my mates. I was so nervous I couldn't eat much lunch. I had no idea what was going on in my bride's mind. She was also having a chilled day with her girls. A few hours before the wedding my groomsmen and I were getting ready together. It was a fun time and very special to have all of them together.

Maddy remembers, "Thinking of my special day, I was very relaxed because we had organized everything beforehand and the ceremony was not until 4.30pm. I had the whole morning to be organized. My mother, my family and I hung out together and that was very special. I was staying in my friend's house, as they have a studio. The bridesmaids were with me there for two nights. We had a lot of fun. My family was on the same property and they stayed in the trailer. This was a special time for me.

"I had breakfast and a relaxing morning. I was so nervous, especially as I had prepared a surprise for Derek. I prepared everything perfectly, but I also asked my other friends to take care of the decorations and sound system. I was nervous about all the details – but it was perfect."

I was excited and also nervous at the same time. I took a few showers because I was getting very sweaty through nerves, but I knew it was going to be special. Organizing a wedding and taking that leap of faith is not always for the faint hearted!

Right after 4 p.m. people were arriving on the beach for the wedding. The sky was beautiful, the ocean was beautiful and the sun was up. There were little waves crashing on the shore making an amazing, quiet noise. It was a dream wedding. Then a few friends came to me and hugged me, saying they were happy to be here. Tears were already coming into our eyes. What was I going to be like when the actual ceremony started? Then at 4pm we drove to the beach. The clock hit 4.30 p.m. and there was no bride. Where was she? I was so impatient. At 4.31 p.m. I was mad because my bride hadn't arrived. I asked Ted, "What time is it now?"

"It is 4.35," he said.

I asked, "Where is the bride?"

He said, "I don't know."

Angels brought me here

We started to listen and then heard someone singing from afar. I kept listening to the music and thinking, *Oh my gosh, what is that?* I had no idea what was going on. I wanted someone to tell me when the bride was walking down the aisle. Then the sound of the music was getting closer and I realized that Maddy was walking down the aisle and signing with her beautiful voice and then I started to cry. Everyone else started to cry as well. There were no dry eyes at all. She was singing the song 'Angels Brought Me Here' and it was just so emotional. Every time I watch the wedding video, I cry again. I'm almost crying here now.

"I wanted to surprise Derek," said Maddy. "I didn't tell him I was going to sing. That was the only way to have that moment together. That's why I made that decision."

"The chorus went:

> *If you could see what I see you are the answer to my prayers.*
> *And if you could feel the tenderness I feel you would know*
> *it would be clear that angels brought me here.*

My bride was singing and holding her father's arm and walking toward me. She kept singing, then when she approached me, she held my hand. I didn't know how she could sing and walk at the same time. I was crying - it was so emotional. "It was hard to not cry, I didn't want to cry because it would mess up the singing," Maddy said, remembering this beautiful time. "However I did mess up a little because it was too emotional, but at the same time very beautiful. In fact everyone was crying!"

The ceremony started after Maddy finished singing. The pastor who was marrying us talked about marriage and introduced us. We sang two worship songs to God that I chose and Maddy agreed, which were

'Oceans' and 'How Great Thou Art'. The presence of the Holy Spirit, God and the angels was so strong that we were all crying so much. What an emotional wedding! After we worshiped the pastor read the Bible. We had my mother reading the verse in the Bible talking about love, which was very special. Then we made the vows and Maddy read her own vows that she wrote. That was gorgeous. Then I started to cry and all the people kept crying.

As the wedding concluded and we were about to walk off the beach, one of my groomsmen, Ted, shouted, "There is a great white shark a few meters from the shore." A few people saw it. It was certainly something that everyone would remember.

Even though I could not see it I could see with God's eyes and feel with my heart the great job that my wife had done and the miracles from God. It just made Maddy and I remember what God told my mother before: that we should not worry, that God would give Maddy the wedding of her dreams.

We all dined together at the reception and we partied together. Maddy and I did our wedding dance. It was beautiful.

Since the wedding, we have not had any fights. Our relationship has become even better. All of those fights were because of the stress. The enemy tried to break us down. Now we have been married for a few years and our relationship is really amazing. I still can't believe I have such an amazing wife.

Maddy's mother added, "It was very exciting and it was the first time I was visiting Maddy in Australia, even though she had lived there for three years. We stayed with the family that Maddy was living with at the time. There was some chaos – renovations were going on that week of the wedding, it was very crazy. I was very nervous before the wedding. I went with Maddy for the last alterations of her wedding dress and that was very special. I was very sad because we were there for three weeks in Australia and only saw Derek twice. But it was the wedding and Derek had his family and friends there as well. I wanted to see Derek so badly but it only happened the day before the wedding. The day of the wedding was very emotional and exciting and I suffered from many nerves. On the day of the wedding I went to the beach and there was seaweed all over the sand and I rake it all up. It took me three hours as I did the whole beach. But it was good for me and my nerves.

"Maddy and I have a very close relationship. We talk mostly every day. So when I get nervous she gets nervous. I didn't sleep the night before the wedding. Also because Maddy and her bridle party were very loud. They were practicing the dance and the music was loud so I couldn't sleep. I was a bit sad that I couldn't understand the whole ceremony because my English wasn't that good. I have been practicing my English more so I can talk to Derek. I always follow them on Facebook and Instagram. I always ask about Derek. Now we are waiting for grandchildren!"

"It feels good to be a married woman," Maddy confessed. "Honestly it feels like we have been married forever. Very quickly I got adjusted to Derek's blindness. For me it doesn't feel like I have a man who is different to other men. There are some things he cannot do. But would a seeing man do these things? I am very handy myself, so it doesn't matter to me. Derek does show his weaknesses and his vulnerability, which is a lovely thing. He is very emotional and can be very open.

"We were ready for a new life together, new challenges for husband and wife. We were committed to support and help each other. We also knew we wanted to share with people that our relationship was a gift from God and we bring all honor to Him. We want to inspire other couples that they can have a beautiful marriage under God's hands. We are forever grateful to God for His grace and all the miracles."

THE WEDDING OF THE YEAR…

In my mind I could not believe how great it was. I was not only excited to be married but appreciating how wonderful it is to be married. I know since then being with someone you love so much and who loves you so much it is the greatest experience ever. Because I know that Maddy is there for me and I am there for her. Since we have been married we so appreciate being together and I can tell that if I knew being married was that good, if a wedding would be that beautiful and so amazing and emotional I would have got married before, not 10 months after I met Maddy. I would have chosen to get married on the first day because the ceremony was so, so, so emotional.

I recommend being married to everyone once they find someone who they love and who is loved in return. But first you do need to find someone who loves you and you love because marriage is not just about you anymore, you have a mission. It's not making your spouse happy because if you have to do this then it means they were not happy before you met your spouse. You have to compliment the happiness. Maddy was happy before I met her but I'm there to compliment and to fill her happiness even more. I was happy before I met her – she met me and she complimented my happiness. So together we are even happier, we are even stronger, we are even closer to God. We are even more prepared to face every single challenge that life brings. Together we can overcome difficulties, overcome limits, we can share experiences and help each other, be there for each other.

Since Maddy and I met we agreed that whenever we have a fight and don't agree with each other, we would never go to sleep at night not talking to each other. It's not that we don't have arguments, although it is rare, but we make God the center of our marriage. We bring everything up to him. We would solve the problem, or if we cannot solve the problem, we would solve this the next day in the light of the day and say sorry to each other, hug each other make each other feel loved and be there for each other before we went to sleep. That is what I love about being married.

CHAPTER 12.

TRAVEL TIME

A short time after we started the movie, I began to travel even more, as a few different multi-national companies were sponsoring me we also traveled to promote the movie. That was the start of me flying around the planet – either for surfing, for shooting, for sponsor promotions, or for movie premieres. This increased after the movie was finished, as I had to do a world tour to show the movie in around 30 countries.

I was becoming really famous in a way I never would have thought in my life. This was really cool, but to be honest, at the same time it was not that good for me. Being famous almost made me divert from the right track I was meant to be on, but it also gave me a lot of opportunities to travel around the world and get to know amazing people and build up great friendships.

I made good friendships, where some of those friends became part of my family. But being famous brought negative connotations as well. It made me walk a little far away from God for a certain period of my life. Even though I would never want to be or try to be arrogant, I could sound a little because I didn't even realize when I was not being nice to people. Looking back, that is a fact of my life that I cannot change.

Everything was just so new to me, so I was not ready and prepared to handle all the extra attention. But fortunately, that was for a short time and I always try to remember that being famous never mattered to me. I never cared about that and I should not want to care about it. All I need to care about is to keep being happy, being humble, to keep building hope in peoples' hearts, to help people to try and overcome challenges and also to show people how to walk by faith. That was my main objective.

Living by faith
During the 'Beyond Sight' world movie tour, we went to several countries and we started to see the impact of God's hand on peoples' lives. Many individuals gave their lives to Jesus after they saw the movie. People would ask me: *What would I hope that people would take away with them after they saw the movie?*

My response was not that they thought I was anything special, but that they would ask themselves, 'Why do I limit myself? What is stopping me from achieving my dreams?' I also hoped that they would take home the necessity of walking by faith and not by what they see.

Many people came to me when I was traveling the world to promote the movie and asked me what can they do to live a life like I do. I specifically remember this guy when I was in Switzerland. After he watched the movie, he came to me and he gave me a hug and said, "Hey Derek, I want to live a life like you do. Just by faith. How can I do it?"

Then I said, "First step, just close your eyes and let's pray." So he did and he understood he could live by faith just by believing by faith. It's all about faith. I saw many situations like this guy. I could write an entire book about this. Many people and a few churches and companies and conferences started to slowly contact me because they wanted me to share at their events. In the meantime I kept travelling and surfing a lot. This was such an amazing time.

I was travelling around the world, exploring the world and going to new places, which was exciting and adventurous. There were a lot of lay-overs in many airports – sleeping on the floor in airports in countries where I didn't even speak the language. That was a challenge for me, but I loved it anyway. Once in Indonesia, I was going to fly from one island to another, so I went to book a flight. Because of a misunderstanding, the airline booked me to somewhere else. I only realized when I landed. Without speaking the language, my friends and I were in this little airport as big as my living room trying to understand what was going on. We had to rent a taxi and drive ten hours across the island in the middle of the bushes with six people in a car, eight surfboards and no food overnight. Those are challenges that come as part of the game of travelling around the world and exploring new things. Yes, it was worth it!

I really love adventure and the feeling of adrenalin and being in danger. I guess that's the way I'm wired. I always think positive. I always think that in the end, everything will be fine. If everything is okay, it means there is still more life to be explored and the end hasn't come.

When I was travelling, people were always very excited to meet me. Whenever I arrived in another country they would say, "That's Derek. Let's shake his hand, let's get a picture, get his autograph and get to know him." I always got a warm welcome when I arrived at a venue because people were so excited to meet me. They wanted to hear how a blind guy can surf. Sometimes I would arrive in countries and the people would not speak any of the languages that I spoke. No one could understand me, but even with the language limitation, my friends and I could feel how joyful they felt to welcome me and spend time with me.

Friends all over the world

When I first went to be a guest of honor in a surf camp in California, it was in the very beginning of my career. My English was not that good and when I arrived there were a bunch of kids and I felt so welcome. Even though I had no idea what they were speaking about, that brought me so much joy. I spent time with them and surfed with them and I learnt that it's not about me or surfing, but it's about sharing joy and happiness and faith with others.

My mind was blown by how well people were welcoming me. That helped me to learn to be a better man, a better person, and how to be more humble. Sometimes I would arrive in certain places and the family would have a big house and the little children would give up their own beds to make me feel comfortable. I always felt so blessed.

I never really enjoyed staying at a hotel very much. I could have had that choice, but I would prefer to stay with people. I liked the home feeling to stay with people. It was not because I could save money; it was because I would have a chance to build up a friendship with someone new – to get to know their hearts and their culture. Most of the people I have become really good friends with. Because of that choice that I made, today I have great friends all over the world.

If I was going to a job somewhere – like a surf trip, sometimes friends of mine would know someone and they would connect me with them. That's how it would happen: connection between friends and others. If I was going to speak in a church in a different country or city, they would ask around in the church if anyone wanted to host me. God always brought the right people into my life at the right moment.

While I really loved Australia, Indonesia, Portugal and Hawaii, the truth is I love every single place. I think that every country is different and they have their own beauty and I appreciate that. They have their own culture, their own people and I always love getting to know the country and experience something new.

Derek's father, Ernesto, commented, "When Derek and I first travelled together, Derek was three years-old and this was the first trip we did together. When travelling with Derek, it was very emotional because for me it was the first time I had been out of Brazil. I saw how tough Derek was. It was very interesting getting into the airport and finding our way to the check-in counter and managing the suitcases and surfboards. I saw that Derek was very smart and independent. It was so wonderful to see how smart he was going through immigration, customs and so on. It just confirmed to me even more how much I could trust Derek. I knew my son would not get lost.

"The first trip we did together was to California. Derek's movie was already out. I was very excited and I could see going to the movie theatre that people were excited to watch the movie. Most of the screenings were sold out and there were huge lines of people trying to buy tickets.

"We did that scenario in a few different cities in California. When the movie was finished, it was very emotional for me to see everyone around Derek and pictures being taken and people asking for autographs. It was really special. I thought there would only be people around Derek's age, but I was surprised to see little kids and people up to the age of around 85 in wheelchairs. They could barely walk, but they wanted to watch the movie.

"Travelling with Derek gave me a chance to meet some surfing celebrities who I had seen on the screen, which was a childhood dream for any surfer. Another trip we did together was when we went to compete in a surf contest in a river very close to the border of Canada. When we got there we were very tired. I asked Derek what time it was and he said it was 11 p.m. and I thought he was making fun of me. I went myself to check the time and it was 11 p.m. That freaked me out because the sun was up and I realized we were in the northern hemisphere and the sun takes longer to set. I said, "Let's jump in the river," but the water was extremely cold because the snow from the mountains was melting into it.

"On this same trip there was a contest in this river and there was a huge crowd watching it. In the meantime, Derek was competing and people were in a stadium around the river and they were screaming and cheering for him. It was wonderful to hear. Watching all of that happening for Derek's life made me cry and feel so proud. On this trip, we were able to talk with some businessmen, some great companies and Derek signed a sponsorship, which was one of the biggest sponsors he had received.

"So I did a few other trips with Derek to some surf contests, as Derek was sponsored by big surf brands. We were very fortunate as we were able to stay right in front of the beach where the waves were breaking and stay at the same hotel with the best surfers in the world, past and present. These were surfers who I only saw in magazines; I was able to meet them in person because of Derek. It was a dream come true for me.

"Between all of the trips I did with Derek, one that was unforgettable and special was that he gave me as a gift when I turned 50 years old. He gave me a present, which was a surf trip to Indonesia with him. To do a trip to Indonesia is a dream of every surfer. Indonesia is a great place for surfing. The waves are perfect, the water is really warm, nice weather, great food, different culture. It's definitely a surf dream for anyone. I was so grateful.

"Derek has been there several times before, so he knew the place and what to expect. But the holiday blew my mind because it is a Third World country and to every single spot we went to surf, there were so many stairs down the cliff, at least about 300, and Derek was doing much better than me in negotiating those steps. He knew where every single step was and every beach and surf spot was. I couldn't believe how clever my child was. It was the same when I rode around on our scooters. Indonesians use scooters all the time. He would tell me where to turn and direct me to the right spot to wherever he needed to go.

"The only thing that he didn't direct me to well was the food, so in 30 days of the trip, I lost 15 pounds. Really, that was perfect for me! It was because I was surfing a lot with him and having so much fun and enjoying the waves of my dreams.

"The trip also gave me a chance to meet my future daughter-in-law, who I loved so much from the beginning. Another time when we travelled together was when Derek did a huge commercial campaign for a large brand. They went to Brazil first to film with Derek, then after a few months they flew Derek and I to Australia to promote the advertisement and launch the campaign. Once more, I was amazed when we got there. There were many TV channels, the biggest in Australia, around Derek to interview him. Many people saw his campaign, as it was on the TV and his picture was printed on the product, so he was well known over there.

"I'm sharing that because it makes every single father proud to see how successful their child is – no matter whether they have anything that could limit them. Hopefully that can help with anyone having problems with their children, so they can see and know that their children can rise up to anything.

"One of the most emotional things on that trip was seeing Derek's pictures on the packaging of the product in the supermarkets."

"Travelling with Derek is always very interesting and there are many benefits," Maddy explained. "For instance, you never have to wait in line, which is very handy. Sometimes we get upgraded to Business Class because he is blind.

One time we had a lot of luggage – surfboards and suitcases and everything else that goes with surfing and travel - so Derek had the trolley with all the cases and I had the surfboards in my hand. He was trying to follow the black lines on the floor, but he would sometimes divert off them. He would often bump into people and when I told him there were people, he would call out, 'Out of the way, 'blind man coming.' People would often stand on the blind lines, not realizing what they were for. Derek has to follow that line and people would be in the way.

"In general when Derek bumps into someone, people are firstly rude, then they apologize when they realize Derek is blind. Once someone said Derek was faking his blindness. The reason he said it was because Derek was on the phone. He was just rude and accused Derek continually.

"Sometimes, Derek puts on clothes that don't match. He will put on shirts with stripes and shorts with dots! I like fashion and I like some clothes that I bought him, but if they aren't comfortable, he won't wear them. He used to say, 'I only want to wear board short. They feel comfortable.' The problem is they were all so bright – fine for the beach but not to go out. Somehow they disappeared. I didn't throw them out, but he still believes I threw them away. I just bought him board shorts that looked like normal shorts. He can feel comfortable, but doesn't look like a clown, especially when travelling."

My mother sometimes found it quite stressful while I was travelling. She explained, "When Derek did travel for the first time, I was so worried. My heart was jumping out of my chest because he had always been around me. All I could do was pray for him all the time and bring his life to God so God would protect him and guide him on the way. The first time that he went on a surf trip, he did not have any money to go. I did not have any money to help him as well, so I rented out my home and stayed with my sister so I could make some money to help cover the cost. It is amazing how God provided so he was able to experience his first surf trip."

Derek's father continued: "After that, he started to make some money with surfing and also with the sponsors. The movie also provided finances so he could not only pay for his surf trip, but also to bring me with him on field travels. It was wonderful how well received I was and also mind-blowing how people love my son. Every single place that I went with him, I could see the love that people would have for him. I was pleasantly surprised that people always made me feel very comfortable.

"People really want to hear how he does things and also people want him to share his favourite stories with them. Derek has made a lot of really good friends around the world."

Bryan Jennings remembers his time travelling with Derek. "Well, producing the 'Beyond Sight' movie with Derek, teaching him English and traveling all over the world together has been so special. We have laughed together, shared our faith with hundreds of thousands of people, surfed many surf spots together, and we have become very close friends. I am so thankful for Derek in my life."

One thing I really love while on my travels is when I'm surfing the crowds at beaches, the local people are really protective of me. When there are other surfers who have come from somewhere else and want to surf in those places, it's harder because they want to protect their wave and their break. But with me, it is just amazing because wherever I go, people want to make sure that I get good waves. They make me feel so welcome – they really respect me. It is something that makes me so grateful to see that people respect me wherever I go and surf. When I'm in the most impossible surfing breaks, even with people who are not from the area, they open the doors for me. They let me surf and they respect me. They want to greet me and shake my hand. It's a wonderful thing to experience. You never know what to expect when you arrive in another country, but the hospitality I have experienced has been amazing and I really appreciate this.

CHAPTER 13.

WHAT KEEPS ME GOING IN LIFE

After my first trip to Hawaii, I came back to my hometown. It was not a good season for surfing, so I was a little bored. I was happy to find something else to have fun with. In fact, I was desperate to do something else for a while. I just wasn't good at sitting still for too long, so I was up for another great challenge.

A new love
When I was about the age of one, I was given a child's skateboard from my father. He has told me that I loved the board and I always tried to ride it, even at that young age. I remember when I was around 15 years-old, when my cousin came to my hometown and he brought his skateboard with him. He let me play with his skateboard and told me that I was going to be good one-day. I certainly liked hearing that. I really wanted to be good at something. I was not sure what it was at that stage, so I just got on with life and did a bit of surfing.

I went on a surfing trip to Hawaii a few years later and when I came home, I met some people who were always riding their skateboards and cruising around on the sidewalk in front of the beach near my home. I thought that would be cool to do. I knew they were there because I could hear the noise of the skateboards rolling around on the ground. I approached them and asked them if I could have a go at this and they immediately send yes. I was so surprised; they were really kind and helpful. So this was exciting, a new adventure.

I started to ride the skateboard on the flat ground. I became so in love with that, then I started to challenge myself to go faster and faster. It was so exciting. I became really close friends with those two guys and today, they are some of my best friends. We are like brothers.

Derek's skateboard friend John said, "When I met Derek, I felt very motivated. Sometimes we have some little issue and it starts to limit us. Even a little headache can control us and limit us. I realized that limitations are made by our own self and our own decisions. We can decide what limits we want in our lives.

Adrenalin junkie
"We started to skate on the flat ground, but I realized that Derek always had something different to push himself ahead. He wanted to go further and push himself a lot. I realized that he had a talent for skateboarding. Derek and our team started to get involved with downhill speed skating, but we never thought that we would actually do this. Especially Derek, as it is so dangerous. But in our minds, when we were just skateboarding on the flat ground, we were imagining all the time skating downhill."

I loved skating so much that I was skating more than surfing. It was such a new thing for me. However, my parents were not too happy about me skateboarding because it can be really dangerous. People have had really bad accidents with that. They were so worried about me. But being the type of guy I am, nothing could stop me from skating, so I slowly started to do downhill speed skating. I was so stoked and incredibly excited about this new journey I was on.

John explained, "One of the things that blew my mind was the development and the evolution that Derek had. It was seriously super quick and fast the way he developed his skills on a skateboard. He's blind and I was thinking, *'How can he develop that quickly? We can't do it – we're not developing that much.'* That always drove people crazy. They couldn't understand how he could do it.

"In a short period, we had the transition from being on the flat ground and playing in little hills, then eventually to some bigger and steeper hills. In a short time we were all competing and Derek was doing the same. He was doing well and proving to everyone his blindness could not stop him."

A new profession?

I started to realize I was taking skating more seriously than I thought. I was becoming very competitive in downhill speed skating. I slowly started to compete with people who could see, which was such a challenge for me. I couldn't even believe myself how good I was doing. People could not believe that I was blind, but I didn't care at all if I was doing good or not. I just wanted to have fun.

In the beginning, when I was starting to embark on my new 'profession' of speed skating, I would go and sleep at my friend's house so we could wake up as early as possible to go skating before the sun came up and it became too hot. My father was not too happy about that at first because he didn't know those two friends very well, but he needed to trust me. He was unsure and very concerned about me doing downhill speed skateboarding. Looking back, I can understand this.

After a few months, I was competing in some local contests in my city. One year later, I was competing at the International Downhill Speed Skateboard World Tour. It was unbelievable, even for me. I was super happy to see the work of God in my life. He was always protecting me from accidents and injuries. I was doing what I loved.

Because of all my skateboarding, I was finally able to do this professionally, going to so many places inside Brazil to compete and also contests overseas. I was living the dream on the skateboard. This gave me a second occupation – after surfing, that is. I was thankful to God for more miracles that he was doing. I was so in love with skateboarding. People would ask me, "Why do you want to skateboard it is so dangerous. Why do you do it?" I would say that I love challenges; they make me stronger, so I keep going. I love and need challenges.

I just kept skating, going around to many contests and getting good results. It was one more tool that God gave to me so I could inspire other people and encourage them. If I'm blind and I can go down the hill really fast on a skateboard, then what can you do if you can see? That is a challenge to those who have sight. A few years later, I was really enjoying life and skating all the time. I was preparing myself to go to the International Skating Championship Awards in California. When we got there, it was summer and the weather was so hot. We had a few days to practice before the contest. I was just so excited – it would be an amazing contest and I believed I could do really well. I was well prepared, training hard for the whole year.

Another skateboarding friend, Heitor, also explained: "The first time that Derek competed in a contest, I took him. It was a contest near our hometown. At that time, we were just adapting ourselves at how to do downhill speed, as we were so new to it. At the very beginning of the contest, we were just practicing and comparing with the other competitors before it started. We were much lower in ranking than the other competitors.

"When the contest began, we started to race even better than we were doing before. So Derek could pass a few bumps, which was a surprise for me and for himself also at how good he was doing. There were around 50 competitors in this contest and Derek remained in the first 15 places. For a blind person that is wonderful, if you think of how many challenges he had to go through. Also Derek was just a beginner in this new sport, but this did not stop him to wanting to be competitive and give his best."

A great disappointment
Unfortunately, the night before the contest started I injured my right foot really badly. I tore the ligaments in my ankle and foot. My friends and I were training for jujitsu and my friend fell on my foot when my foot was sideways. I don't know why I was doing jujitsu before a contest. I guess I didn't stop to think about it. He was very heavy and my foot twisted in a bad way. I started to scream so loudly that people thought I was dying. Immediately, my foot became so swollen. I said to everyone, "I broke my foot." They straight away brought ice and they helped me until we got to the hospital. I couldn't believe it.

So that was it. The dream of participating in the most important competition in my skateboarding career was destroyed. I couldn't believe it – after all my training. I had to watch everyone else competing while my friends were caring for me, as I could not walk. I had to fly back home in a wheelchair. Since then, I have never gone back to riding the skateboard. I gave it my very best. I could not even surf for a couple of months.

When I thought that I was well recovered from my injury, I went surfing with my dad. When I got on the first wave and took off and set my foot on my board, it was so painful. I was about to cry because I couldn't handle that much pain. I was pounded by the waves. They were smaller waves, but powerful and as I was in so much pain I could not swim away. So I was hampered in every way and this upset me greatly. Finally, someone who was surfing helped me to get to the shore and the lifeguards drove us back home.

So I had to handle being blind, which was not too much of a problem because I had grown up with this, but I also had to handle not being able to skateboard or surf because of my injured foot. That was a double hit to me. I felt so useless and so disabled because I couldn't do anything. I couldn't be independent like I once was. I was fairly unhappy for some time. I was asking myself, *Why did I hurt myself that bad? Why did it have to happen to me?* Then my answer was, *It is on purpose from God to see if I would still trust and have faith.* Then I realized I could be happy, even if I had an injured foot and I couldn't surf or skate. That was a good place to get to. I had such peace. That's not an easy decision to make, but once you arrive, there is such freedom.

So life kept going and I continued to praise God that my foot was getting a little better, but since the injury, even though after examinations and medication, my foot never became the same again. Even today, I feel pain every now and then, especially if I'm doing skateboarding downhill because it requires a lot of pressure on the front foot – the right one that was injured. It's hard for me to do this.

Heitor continued, "I remember one contest, one of the first few that Derek was involved in. There was a big crowd watching the contest along the track going down the street. Derek did this great overtake, leaving behind an amazing skater who had a huge chance of winning this contest. Right in front of us, after Derek overtook that guy, there was this big turn that we had to do, like an S. You have to choose the right spot on the track to make your turn so you make the distance shorter, then you gain time and speed. That big crowd was cheering and screaming Derek's name out loud. That gave me butterflies and goose bumps. It was one of the best feelings I have had. Until today, every time I remember that time, I can feel that sensation and it gives me a wonderful feeling in remembering it."

A new challenge

Although I miss skateboarding and performing better, as I always aim to do, I'm still a very happy and grateful person and always thinking positive. Nowadays, I only go skateboarding if I need to do any presentations or any filming for campaigns, or any other type of work that would involve skateboarding, but my passion for sports that is on boards was not for only skateboard and surf. There was always something else that I wanted to learn since I had heard about it: snowboarding.

When I was younger, I had heard about snowboarding, but I never really wanted to learn it until after I was already skateboarding. Then I realized that my passion was to do sports that would involve any type of boards. So this was good; I was really stretching myself. I wanted to experience everything I could. Scott, a friend of mine from California who was not only a great surfer, but also snowboarder, always told me I should know how to do snowboarding, that it would be very exciting and challenging for me. I said I always wanted to learn it, but I didn't know if I was willing to deal with the snow and the falls. Over the years, he kept telling me that one day he would teach me. Then a few other people asked me if I had tried snowboarding. So I felt like it might be something I would like to try one day. Maybe that was a message for me. I really was willing to try anything.

A 'mammoth' introduction to snowboarding

One day, Scott decided to take me to the mountains on a weekend so he could teach me how to snowboard. We drove there, which was around six hours from our home. Scott's wife and children also came, as did Maddy. It was going to be a packed trip. A few days before we drove up to the mountains, Scott got all the gear ready and he explained to me very carefully what everything was for. I tried the snowboard on to see if it was the right fit for me. In that moment, I had an amazing feeling of adrenalin. I was always thinking about how the snow would feel under my feet. I was trying to understand in my mind how that would feel.

We finally got into Mammoth Mountain, a city in California. The funny thing was that it was in the middle of the summer and they still had a lot of snow. It was very slushy, though. The first day I attempted snowboarding, it was Maddy's birthday. It was the first time that Maddy had spent her birthday in the snow. It was July and summer and normally there is never snow in July, but we were blessed. Snow surrounded us on the mountain and it made the holiday a very special time. I wanted to make sure Maddy was happy on her birthday. Everything went very well.

Then we woke up on the day we were going up the mountain to snowboard. I didn't have much breakfast. I got to the mountain; we had our gear and I went for my first run, obviously on the smallest hill in the ski resort. That's how I had to start. I did my first run and we were taking it very slow. Scott was leading me with his hands and talking to me so I could be guided down the mountain. It was a lot of fun and easy, particularly as we were taking it slow. We took it very easy the first day, then I had one more day of snowboarding before we drove back home. So the second day was a little more challenging, as I always want to go further and try to push myself over my limits. I tried to go down on a little higher run than the one from the day before. I made it a few times, but I also had some bad experiences. I ran over some people and felt really bad doing this. That was the first run downhill. The hill was really small and I crashed into a tree. I also crashed on the rocks and I fell off the chair lift. Because I was late trying to get off the lift, I didn't jump out at the right moment. Not a good start, but at least I was trying. I wanted to master this.

Those were my first experiences with the snowboard. I was very sore afterwards and I also had a few wounds. At that time, I saw that if I wanted to proceed with snowboarding, it would not be easy. I was so grateful to Scott to teach me and to dedicate his time. Oh, but it was a challenge and I am used to challenges, right?

Scott stated, "For a while, Derek and I had surfed together and we had a good connection in surfing. I could be his guide and it worked for us. We decided to give that same relationship a try for snowboarding. On the first morning, we called ahead to the mountain to the Adaptive Ski Program and they have instructors who teach people with disabilities. I thought, 'That's great we'll get an instructor.' We got there and they said, "Sorry everyone's gone, all the instructors have left for the season."

I said, 'Could you give us the blind skier jackets? At least that way people will know my friend is a blind skier and I am helping him.'

"Derek had no fear and called out, 'Come on Scott, the two of us can do it.' We started out on the beginner's slopes and I was helping him. Within four hours, we were on the regular runs, going downhill holding hands and making turns like other skiers. Within half a day, Derek was snowboarding and laughing and when one of us would fall, the other one would go down also. It was certainly challenging. By the second day, Derek was 'rocking and rolling'. It was such a neat moment for me. I could see Derek take on something new. He had never seen a snowboard, a boot - anything. When I gave him the board, I had to show him how everything worked. Standing up was another challenge. I had to describe the sport to him, having to start from scratch. He was totally into it. He didn't want to look good - he just wanted to do it."

The following winter, we went back to the mountains and that was so much fun. I could overcome those challenges and bad experiences that happened on the last trip. Then on that weekend, which was my second trip, I pushed myself and with Scott's help, I could do much better. I had so much freedom. I was snowboarding down the mountains very fast. It was so amazing to see not only how God leads me on the waves, but also on the snow as well. I was in seventh heaven. It's always a wonderful feeling when you overcome obstacles and achieve what you set out to do.

I always bring all the glory to God in every single thing I do. People may think I am a super hero, but I am definitely not. It's just a fact that if we believe and have faith, we can accomplish anything. We should never let traumas and bad experiences hold us back. What I do is always use those experiences and challenges to strengthen me and push me forward.

The only thing that can stop and hold you back is yourself. The same way you can dream about something, you can actually do it. You just need to be strong, believe in yourself, choose the right path and not give up in achieving whatever you want.

CHAPTER 14.

MY DOG - MY PRECIOUS COMPANION!

I always thought of myself as a very independent person. I was always happy using my walking cane for anything I needed to do. I didn't need anything else to help me. Life was good and I was making my way around brilliantly. Nothing or no one was going to stop me or get in my way - or so I thought, until something beautiful – like my guide dog - came my way.

I could go anywhere I wanted, anytime I wanted to, with my walking stick. I could fly to different countries on my own, go on trains, ferries and buses on my own. If I needed to carry surfboards and suitcases, I could still manage it. I was totally in control. But on the other hand, even though the walking cane is useful, it is only an object detector. I would still bump into things and people accidentally and anything in front of me. Then I would be in some trouble, it was not so pleasant if people abused me.

However, since I was very young, my grandmother kept telling me I should get a guide dog. I always liked that idea. I was not someone who always loved dogs a great deal, but I didn't mind them. I had never really grown up with them, so I was a bit nonplus about the idea, really. I wasn't sure how I would handle a dog. It seemed like it would end up being a lot of work! I never went too deep on the subject of a dog with anyone, but often someone would ask me, "Why don't you get a guide dog?" I was happy with my walking stick at that time. At some point, I actually thought it was not nice that people made dogs work.

The first time I got to know about guide dogs a little more was when I was in Australia doing a speech at a blind society. They also had a guide dog program, so they brought one of their guide dogs in training to meet me so I could have an experience of how the program works. I loved it. I had a beautiful experience for a few minutes and I was already in love with the idea of having a guide dog. I immediately told my wife and she was so excited. She said, "That's so cool, maybe one day you should get a guide dog." I was beginning to hope someday I would.

A suprise from Maddy

A few months later, I was just at my home and I realized my wife was spending a long time on her computer, which was unusual, and printing a lot of papers. She would not tell me what she was doing, which made me so mad. But anyway, I let her do her thing. I thought she was checking some surfboards for my birthday, which was coming up soon. I was hoping this was the case! I really wanted a new board. Hopefully this was the surprise.

One day I woke up and my wife was getting ready to leave earlier than usual. I asked her what she was doing and she said, "You have to trust me. Bye."

I thought, *Oh my goodness, what is going on with that girl? I cannot understand women.* I'm sure I'm not the only guy who says this! After my head was in a spin about all of this, Maddy came to me and said, "Hey babe, I was not meant to tell you, but I wanted to give you a surprise for your birthday. I want to bring you a guide dog. Do you remember all those times I was typing and printing and you were annoyed at me? I was preparing your application to receive a guide dog. I even contacted your eye doctor in Brazil without you knowing.

"I received from her your eye situation report, as they required. But I will not be able to surprise you on your birthday. I had no idea how the program works, as they are really strict and they need you to have a doctor's appointment and have some basic exams. As I couldn't do that, I had to tell you the whole situation now. Also I wanted to bring the guide dog to you at your party, but that would never happen because if your application is accepted, you have to go to class and stay in class for three weeks in training with the dog. I did try my best to surprise you, but I had no idea how it worked."

I said, "Honey, you are amazing. You are so awesome." I was so happy and excited. I loved the idea of getting my own dog. Normally, when you do an application to receive a guide dog, it can take at least around six months to one year to be approved and receive the dog. Sometimes it can take up to two years. I did go to the doctor and do all the exams required. We completed all the paperwork that was necessary. We put together some videos of my daily life: how I was walking around. I sent in the application and the board made an appointment for an interview with me, which took over an hour. They told me that within 15 days they would get back to me with an answer.

The next day my phone rang and it was Guide Dogs of America, which is the school to which I had applied to and I thought they must have forgotten to ask me something else. They gave me the great news that my application was accepted and I was going to receive my new guide dog. The next class available was going to be in seven months' time, as they had only one class coming up in less than a month, but that class was already full and they were going to close the building for renovations. So I had to wait.

They did ask me for my availability within in a few weeks, just in case any of the students who were attending the next class happened to cancel. Then I could be on the list. I said, "Yes, you can call me and I will go."

They said, "Don't have too much expectation. It's not normal someone would give this up."

I said, "Okay." So I was all set to come to the class seven months from that time. A few weeks later, I received a call from the association stating that the class had started the day before and they had one student who could not attend at the last moment. So they invited me to come if I was available. I started to jump up and down in the house and called my wife and I told her. She couldn't believe this. It was a real miracle.

So within a month, I prepared my application, I did my interview, I was approved and I received my dog. Wow, that was so fast. I couldn't believe it. It is so amazing how God works. Some people take up to two years to get their guide dog, but my wife and I were so anxious and we really couldn't wait for even seven months. It was always in my mind how my life would be with a guide dog. So after I received their phone call, my wife cancelled her working shift because she needed to drive me to the Guide Dogs of America campus in LA. So we quickly packed up my suitcase, as I was going to stay there for three weeks, then we jumped in the car and drove for two hours together. We were so excited and so happy.

Once we got to the campus, we were so well received and welcomed. Then someone came to receive us and there was a guy holding this black Labrador. All the time when we did the application, Maddy was telling me about the pictures of the dogs and she was hoping and wishing I would get a German Shepherd or a black Labrador. To be honest, I was more excited to get a Labrador than a German Shepherd, but it didn't really matter. At least I was getting my own dog.

When we saw the dog, Maddy said, "Oh my gosh, it's a beautiful black Labrador." We thought that dog was going to be my dog, but it was the actual handler's blind dog. Maddy was so hopeful she was going to be able to meet my dog when she dropped me that day to start my training, but unfortunately for her, that is not how it works. We only get to meet our dog on the third day. This is because the instructors have to get to know each student because each student has a different personality and they have to be matched with the right dog. That's how it works and it definitely makes sense. You want a dog that is compatible with your character and personality.

The first day of training, we walked just with our walking stick with the instructor so they could assess our mobility and how fast we could walk. On the second day of training, they started to do something which is called 'juno walk'. That means the instructor is holding the harness in the same position as the dog would be, so we get to know how it works. The training is really strict and functional, but it really works and we learn so much.

On the first few days before we are matched with a dog, we get to know some other dogs and we do some heeling work with them. You only have the dog on a leash and you just heel them inside the building, so you start to get a feeling for how it is with the dog. It is so interesting and emotional how the training goes. I was constantly very teary at the thought of having my own dog and it being part of our family. I would often sit and cry at this wonderful opportunity. God is so good.

Along with those practice-training sessions, we also had a lot of lectures about everyday things we were going through. We also had speech training given by the instructors. Finally, the third day is when we meet our dogs. Before that, we were all really nervous. I never thought I would be that nervous to meet my dog. Honestly, I was so anxious. It felt like for me my wife was about to give birth. I knew it was going to be something entirely different, but it was so exciting at the same time. I just couldn't wait. *What dog would I receive, would the dog really love me and work with me? How would I cope when I went home?* All these thoughts were going through my mind.

Serenity

We all met our dogs after lunch at the end of the third day. Before then, in the morning there was still training going on, each student working with their own instructor. Then we went back to the campus. We had lunch, we had another lecture and then each student went back to their bedroom. So the instructors recommended that we leave the door unlocked and just sit on the couch so they can just walk in with the dog to introduce them to us. I was sitting and I could listen to the other students receiving their dogs, as I can hear really well and that made me so excited.

When I got to the school on the second day, I met this beautiful German Shepherd and I was so in love with him. I told all the trainers, "I hope my dog is a German Shepherd." I was so in love and I wanted one. So I didn't want anything else. I was calling my wife over the phone saying, "I hope I get a German Shepherd." In my mind I was always going to get a male dog. I always wanted a male. This was how I was thinking.

So there I was sitting in my room and Kim, the instructor, opened the door and walked into my room and I could hear four paws touching the floor. My heart was beating fast; the time had come. It sounded so exciting and she said, "I have a friend for you. I'm just going to let her sniff around first. It is a female yellow Labrador." She told me her name is Serenity, so she let the dog come to me and she gave me the leash and immediately this beautiful dog was cuddling, licking and sniffing me. It was the most incredible time.

Our bond was just starting to develop, then the instructor left so we could have a few hours on our own. I was just patting Serenity, getting to know her. I realized that she had amazingly soft ears. She was just the cutest dog ever. I was definitely so in love with her. I could tell that she had a lot of energy and she loved to play and she was listening and respecting her commands very well.

After a few hours together, it was time to give our dogs dinner and relieve them. That was the first time that I fed her. The instructor showed us the amount of food and water to give them. We set the bowl of food down. We told our dogs to sit and only eat after we said 'okay'. Serenity only ate after I gave her the okay. I was surprised how fast she ate. Then we relieved the dogs and it was our time to go to the main room in the building so the students were able to introduce their guide dogs.

The training kept going and I remember the first time I had Serenity in a harness. She was dragging me forward because she was fast and very excited, but always navigating safely with me. Well, I guess she was just like me: fast and excited about everything. We were well matched.

According to what the instructors were saying, I was developing really well with the training. I felt good about this. After each five days of training, the instructor would sit with each student to give them a report on what they needed to concentrate on and how they were doing. Praise God, my reports were always great.

So the training kept going – we were having such a fun time. Each day there were different challenges, but the bond was developing. The graduation day was soon to come. One day before the graduation, we were told if we had passed the test to graduate. Our class started with nine students and six students were able to graduate. The other three were going to have in home training.

Graduation

We all knew the graduation day would be so emotional. Each student was going to meet the people who raised the dogs before they actually go into training to become a guide dog. I really appreciate them because it must be something so hard to do – having to then let them go. I am sure it would be similar to raising a child and giving them up to be adopted by someone else. They do fall in love with their puppies and they stay with the puppies for 15 months, so they teach the puppies the basic commands.

On the graduation day, I met Gwen and Bob Whitson from Guide Dogs of America, who had raised Serenity. They came into my bedroom and I had Serenity with me. She was so excited to see her parents, as she hadn't seen them for three months due to being in intensive training all that time. It was such a wonderful reunion.

Then we went to the building where the graduation was to take place. Each student had a chance to share and each of the puppy raisers also shared and it was incredibly emotional. There were many tears flowing because it is such a great connection.

Then it was time to come home with my beautiful guide dog. I got home and the first thing I did was to take Serenity to the beach so she got to know what I love the most. When I took her to the beach she was so excited and happy, but she didn't show a lot of interest to jump into the water. She just liked to hang and play near to the shore. I was a little bit sad because I always hoped my dog would love to swim with me, but

I understood her and I knew that in time, she would start to enjoy the ocean and feel comfortable. It was still such a special time with her on the beach.

Living with Serenity and spending time with her was definitely challenging, as it was such a new environment for her. It's normal they would make a mistake every now and then and also because they are bonding with their handler. It's a big adjustment. Sometimes it can be a bit frustrating because you expect your dog would always be perfect. And it was no different with me; I went through so many challenges.

As the time went on Serenity would do better and better. Our bond was growing faster than normal. Everyone was so surprised at how good she was doing. I was really surprised. The perfect bonding for a guide dog and a handler can take at least one year because you are starting to get to know each other until you become a perfect team.

Very quickly I was 100% sure Serenity had changed my life, especially in terms of mobility. With her I had freedom, I don't bump into anything anymore. I find my way easier and I'm happier. I say that she is a gift from God into my life. She was chosen from God by His hand to me. I did believe I got the best dog for me.

CHAPTER 15.

THE RUSH OF RIDING BIG WAVES

"After seeing Derek on the big waves, no-one else in the world could claim to be a big wave surfer. Derek is the ultimate big wave rider, no one else. It's the most incredible thing seeing him in big wave surfing."
Big wave Brazillian surfer Ricardo Dos Santos

Since I had started to surf, I not only wanted to be a normal surfer, but I would always try to chase the best waves. Something that I learnt from my father when he started to teach me was that I should always wait not only for the best wave, but also to try and get the biggest waves. Always wait for the huge set. Well, that set me on a course for my destiny – to ride the biggest waves I could find.

Over the years in my career, my passion for surfing was getting stronger and stronger and every time I would surf, I wanted to get out of the water knowing I had ridden the biggest wave of the day. But it's not something that is always so easy because many surfers want to ride the biggest wave, so there is usually some competition. That's how my desire for big waves started. It was just something that drove me to this.

Surfing in my hometown at the beach break would be something that was always exciting, especially when we would check the forecast and I knew there would be a new swell coming. When the weather would change and the wind would turn from north to south, I would know that the next day the waves would be a lot of fun – as well as challenging!

The night before those days, I would always feel nervous and anxious, but also excited. Sometimes I would not even sleep at night. My emotions and thoughts would run all over the place, but when the sun would rise the next morning, I would go to the beach and enjoy surfing the waves. One of the worst things for me is when you create a lot of expectation. You know the surf would be really good and you have the right equipment, the right surfboard, the conditions are perfect, you are in the right spot, but unfortunately sometimes it can turn out not to be your day. Actually, occasionally it turns out to be the opposite from what I would think and expect: I would get no waves, I get pounded and I surf really badly. There were many situations like that. It was something that I struggled with a lot. I would get really angry with myself and that would get me down and make me upset. I don't know why I reacted like this, but on the other hand, if it was a day when I was ripping and surfing really well, I would get out of the water super happy, super excited. I would be someone else – the real me.

Another broken board

There was one day I had a new surfboard and I was so stoked to try it out. Right in front of my home in Brazil, the waves were quite big and closing out a lot, but I still wanted to paddle out and challenge myself, even though it was really dangerous and not always worth it. But being the person I am, I still paddled out and right before I got on the outside, a huge set of waves were approaching me and I had to duck dive. Once they closed right on me and my surfboard got broken into two pieces. I immediately had to paddle into the shore and I was in tears because it was the only surfboard I had. That just showed me I should have listened to my friends when they told me not to paddle out. A good and big lesson to learn! However, I did manage to acquire another board, which eased the pain.

I still had that desire to always ride bigger waves, which was for me something around six feet. That was already big for me. In my hometown in our daily lives, the surf would be always around between three and four feet. On the days when it was around six or maybe eight feet, it was for us quite big. That is what I was always looking for in my surfing life – to go bigger and bigger. So, I kept going with my surfing and I accomplished a few dreams. I surfed one of the most dangerous waves on the planet, which was Pipeline in Hawaii. That was incredible, but it still that wasn't enough for me. I wanted to go further and bigger. That tells you how crazy I was. I wanted to surf bigger than Pipeline.

My first tow in

I remember one day, I was in Rio de Janeiro in Brazil with Carlos Burle, a big wave surfer. He has ridden some of the biggest waves in the world several times in different spots. I met Carlos when I was participating in a TV show where they asked me if I would take the challenge of learning how to be towed in. 'Tow in', for those who don't know, means there is a jet ski with a long rope attached to the ski, where you hold on at the end of the rope with a handle and you have your board under your foot over the water and the guys tow you into the waves. It's much like waterskiing. The reason that there is a tow in when the waves are a bit bigger is because just by paddling out, surfers would not be able to catch the waves because the speed of the waves are much faster than our speed when we paddle.

Well, I did take the challenge to learn to tow in. The waves were not big on that particular day. The idea was not about the size of the waves; it was about the challenge of being towed in, which is something really hard, especially when you cannot see. It's totally different to normal surfing. You have to learn how to hold onto the rope, how to stand up on the towed surfboard, which is different. It's much heavier. There are straps where you have to put your foot in, so it was a new world for me. But I was so enthusiastic I went out into the ocean to experience this.

There was a big crew to help me. They set up skis to help, but they also brought out a boat that could give me support because they knew the challenge would be long and difficult. There was a boat to give me support and I started to try it out. I tried for so many times and then I couldn't make it, not even standing on the board, to start to ski on the ocean, which is the first step. I would fall down all the time, even though they were explaining perfectly the right way to do it. After trying for many hours on that day, Carlos and all the crew decided it would be better to stop, take a rest and try again the following day. I accepted their decision, as I was about to give up myself. I never thought that tow in would be so hard to do.

I then went back to the hotel where I was staying. I had a good rest and I got ready for the next morning. Instead of taking me into the ocean, to make it easier they took me inside a harbor, where the water obviously was more flat and there were no bumps that could make my life harder when I was trying to learn how to ski. The idea to take me there I thought was a bit stupid because there were no waves, but it was actually smart because it was not about just getting the waves. I first needed to go step by step and learn how to ski. It was a beautiful day and nice and warm. I had my dad with me to encourage and help me.

Then I started to try and ski on the water. It was getting much easier, as it was so glassy and still. After trying a few times, finally I was able to stand on a board and ski behind the jet ski. Then I practiced there for a few hours. Everyone was so happy and I was as well, that I could accomplish the task. I was also glad that I didn't give up because if I had, I am sure I would not have been able to ride seriously big waves.

After I was able to ski on the flat water, they took me into the ocean and I tried to learn to ski on the water, which was still very hard. I couldn't get up and stand on the surfboard straightaway like I could on the harbor, however I did find it a little easier after practicing in the flat water. That was a challenge in itself! After trying a few times, I was finally able to ski behind the jet ski and the next challenge came, which was to get on the wave. But apparently it was an easy day and the waves were quite small, but they were still perfect. So I tried a few times.

Some waves I would fall off straight away after being towed. Some other waves I would lose direction because with the tow in, it has much more speed than normal surfing and that would make me lose orientation. I would not know where I was on which spot of the wave. That just made my life very hard and very confusing, but I was still able to catch one wave and ride it to the end. That challenge finally paid off as I was learning how to tow in. The film company was able to show that on the TV show for the whole country of Brazil. It brought me a lot of credibility and that made my surf career stronger, but I still kept within me the desire, especially after that, to get some bigger waves. A few months later, I was back in Rio to watch and do some activities at the World Championship Tour of surfing, known as the World Surf League. One of those contests was in Rio.

THE RUSH OF RIDING BIG WAVES

Am I crazy?
One day in Rio, they didn't run the contest because the waves were too big and closing out, so only the people doing tow in surfing were out there. Carlos was also there, as he lives in Rio. Then he contacted me and asked if I wanted to do some tow in. I said, "Why not." I wanted to be involved in everything. We prepared to do it and we got the surfboards. We got the life vests and we drove to the harbor where the ski was. We had a whole crew of people filming that because everyone thought it was not normal that the blind surfer wanted to do tow ins because the waves were too big. They all thought I was crazy. Maybe I was!

Then we got the skis and Carlos started to drive the ski towards the ocean from the harbor. He told me, "Hey Derek, you have to hold onto me very strongly as we have to go through where the harbor meets the ocean and there are a lot of waves breaking. There will be rocks on both sides of the channels and you cannot fall off at all." I did hold on very carefully. There was a lot of adrenalin flowing as I went through that channel. It was really fun and I always love taking high risks. Well, I guess everyone knew that about me by that time.

Once we were out there in the ocean, Carlos very carefully chose the right waves to put me on. I knew that day I would get the biggest waves I had ridden, so I got one wave. It was quite big and powerful, but it was not the wave of the set that I really wanted. But it gave me a lot of confidence to try and get a bigger one for the day. We were out in the ocean for a few more hours. It was hard to decide which waves to ride, however Carlos did choose for me a big, clean wave to ride. He told me, "Derek this is going to be a big one. Be prepared."

I was feeling so anxious and I had butterflies. That feeling of nerves and adrenalin was taking over me, so I rode the wave and when the wave closed out, I got totally pounded, and when I got back to the surface I thought, *I love it. I want to ride only big waves*' That wave was around 10 to 12 feet.

A few months later, I was back in Hawaii and Carlos was also there for the surf season. He took me to get some waves with the ski and he did tow me on a few waves. I was definitely very nervous because surfing in Hawaii is extremely powerful and dangerous, but I did get some waves on that day. It was a little bigger than the last waves I rode in Rio. I was taking it step by step on these big waves. I was finding my way.

A few times I would do some tow ins, either with Carlos or some other surfer. Each time I would get bigger and bigger waves. It was very challenging and exciting for me. I was definitely keen and willing to try out surfing Jaws in Maui and Nazaré in Portugal one day, but only a few people believed I could make it. Many people would not even listen to what I was saying. They thought I was joking or crazy. They didn't know me well enough that any time I had a dream in my life, I would work really hard until I made it. I was very determined and still am. I won't let anything stop me. That is the character and personality that has been put within me as a gift.

There were many sessions of tow-ins on huge surfing days in Rio and also in Oahu in Hawaii. I had a chance to meet Garrett McNamara, who is a big wave surfer who lives in Hawaii. We got to know each other at the beach. He was really inspired by my story and I was really glad and blessed to meet the surfer who owns the record of the biggest wave ridden on earth at the time of writing, which was a 78 feet wave in Nazaré in Portugal. Even though I met Garrett, who is an amazing guy, I never mentioned that I wanted to surf Nazaré because I was afraid I would scare him away. I really wanted to surf Nazaré, as I knew the biggest waves would be there. Yes, everyone did think I was crazy, but that didn't matter.

'God's Rock'

One month before my wedding, I left my fiancé in Germany and I was back in Hawaii again for the surf season. A friend of mine contacted Garrett and asked him if he wanted to take me to do some tow-ins on the next swell that was going to come. Garrett said, "Yes of course, bring the boy over. The waves will be great right in front of my house. It's a perfect left hand point break for Derek."

So as you can imagine, I could not sleep that night. I was so thrilled; my emotions were running rampant. I knew it would be a huge day for me. I woke up the next morning and went to Garrett's house with such great anticipation. He already had the skis all prepared on the sand waiting for me. He had the guy to drive the ski who would be in charge of the rescue. He had another ski prepared to take out a cameraman. To be honest, I was so scared and my heart was pounding. The waves were huge. I was all the time asking how big the waves were and they were telling me they were around 20 feet.

My friend Bruno Lemos, who introduced me to Garrett and who was going to film as well, was explaining to me every single detail. He was telling me that right in front of the take off, there were some rocks that were pointing out of the water when the wave was forming. He told me I should not worry. Even if I would fall off on the take off, it would not be easy to hit those rocks, as they were quite far away, but it still drove me crazy, as I just couldn't see. I was not sure where exactly I was. Now that was scary!

The name of that break is 'Devil's Rock'. When I heard that, I immediately started to call it 'God's Rock'. Before jumping on the skis to go out there, I prayed to God and asked for protection and to send me some good waves, so I jumped on the ski with Garrett and I told him to get me a small wave first and he did. He put me on this perfect wave and

I rode for so long. Then again and again he would be towing me in to bigger and bigger waves.

I was already a little tired as I was getting many waves and they were huge. To me they seemed like monsters. I told Garrett, "Let's wait for a big set," and so he did. When it came, he towed me in and it was a perfect big left-hander, which I rode for so long, all the way to the channel. Everyone was so happy and their minds were blown with what I could do. Garrett at that point already knew I wanted to surf Nazaré one day after I rode those waves, which are nothing compared to Nazaré, but Garrett came to me and said, "I'm willing to one day take you to surf at Nazaré." I was so excited and happy and blessed that he was willing to do that with me. I mean it really is a big responsibility and I was so grateful.

So we got out of the water. It was a long day of surfing. After that, I felt so tired and so weak because I had never had an experience like that before. Unfortunately I ended up falling sick in Hawaii. After a few days of not eating at all, having high fever and feeling weak, I then started to feel better. Fortunately it was just a cold and nothing more sinister. I finally got better and I went back to surfing normal waves in Hawaii. Tom Carroll was also in Hawaii and he was going to surf Waimea Bay the next day and he asked me if I wanted to come with him. Did I want to come for a surf?! Waimea Bay is famous for very powerful and big waves that break on the north shore of Oahu. It has a perfect, huge right hand that breaks along the bay and you have to ride bigger boards and very thick ones. They are called 'guns'. Guns give you enough speed to jump on the wave and take off.

So Tom Carroll and I were surfing and he let me use one of his inflatable life vests and he showed me how to inflate it in case I got pounded by waves. The way it works is there is some compressed air inside a tube in the life vest and some strings you can pull and it inflates with the air. This also projects you up from the bottom to the top of the ocean. Right before we jumped in the water I said to Tom, "Tom, I'm sure I will know how to use it if I need as you showed me what to pull to inflate it, but can I please try it out before we go in the water to make sure I'm doing the right thing?"

Tom said, "Go ahead." Then I pulled the string and nothing happened. He said, "Pull strong." I pulled hard and nothing happened. Tom then said, "Let me try this." When he checked this, he realized that it was empty. Realizing that this could have been dangerous for me, he said, "I'm so sorry."

I said, "Don't worry, all good." He replaced this and we were ready to go. Thank goodness I tried it before entering the water! It was Tom and I and a few other friends who paddled out that day. The friends were also going to help me when I needed some assistance. At Waimea Bay, there is a huge shore break to get past before you can paddle out to the breaking waves. Fortunately I could make it, but the shore break pounded some of our friends, so they took longer to get through. When I got out there, I tried for so long to get a wave. There was a lot of water moving, a lot of pressure that would hold you and not allow you to take off. I tried several times for over an hour, until Tom and another friend decided I should try a bigger board, which should help me to have more power to get on the wave. So I switched surfboards with my friend and I tried to paddle for another wave. I could then get a few big waves by paddling. but not being towed in.

After the first few waves, Tom and I waited for a big set and together we rode this amazing right-hander. We were pretty much riding the same wave and celebrating together. We were so excited for that accomplishment. I was so grateful to God and that also helped me to increase my faith even more. That trip to Hawaii was going to end and I was to go back to my fiancé and we were getting married in a couple of weeks. I was taking with me a decision of definitely becoming a big wave rider. I knew it would be a huge challenge and I would have to face many obstacles, but I was ready for the challenge.

"Derek always told me he wanted to ride big waves, but I didn't think it would happen, and especially so quickly," Maddy said. "He had a friend, Garrett McNamara, and Derek said to me, "It's happening." *What did he mean by that? I definitely had my suspicions.*

"Then Derek went to Hawaii and they started to surf big waves in front of Garrett's house where he lived in Hawaii. At that time, I was in Germany. We weren't married then, just engaged. I was a bit worried, but it wasn't that I was really scared because I knew God would protect him. I knew I didn't have to worry. Well, not too much!"

Bruno Lemos explained: "Big wave surfing has gotten really popular in the last few years. I think Derek says that the big wave surfers are more famous and more respected and maybe he wanted that for himself. But I think the real reason was that he possibly wanted to overcome his limitations. This is the only reason I think he wanted to ride big waves, as it is really dangerous. When you desire something, you see and you want that, but for him it is because he is very courageous.

"Something attracted him to surf big waves and that is intriguing for me and many people. *Does he know what he's getting into?* However, we all respected that and I approached Garrett and told him that Derek wanted to surf big waves. Garrett said he would put him on the big waves after a couple of years, but Garrett didn't know if he could do it again. Perseverance, determination, courage; that is something that is hard to explain. Only Derek knows why he is doing that. That has always intrigued me. Why? The other aspect is how well he did riding those. We surfed with Tom Carroll in Waimea, Hawaii and Derek managed to pull that off."

My desire for big waves was definitely out there. Everyone knew it, but not everyone approved of it. Many people thought that it was crazy, but it was what I wanted to do. I knew that in my heart. This was my destiny and I had the faith to trust God.

CHAPTER 16.

MY DESTINY – NAZARÉ AND JAWS

What was I thinking? These waves were like tsunamis. I knew this is what I wanted to do, but… most people would have thought I was crazy. Well maybe… just a little? But I couldn't stop until I rode the biggest wave in the world. I previously had many challenges and getting involved with tow-ins to be able to surf some big waves with Carlos, Garrett and Tom Carroll. I was already thinking all the time how it would be to surf Jaws in Hawaii and Nazaré in Portugal.

Another movie?
The crew that I worked with who were filming my adventures came up with an idea about doing another movie about myself chasing the biggest waves on the planet. What was I thinking? Then we started to put those ideas together, but we knew it would be a challenge because only a few people would want to get involved with that project and I definitely couldn't blame them.

So we contacted Bryan Jennings, who made my first movie 'Beyond Sight' and we asked if he wanted to be involved and work on a new movie with us. He immediately said, "Are you crazy? You want to surf Jaws and Nazaré?"

I said, "Yes, I do."

He said, "Okay, it's your choice, but I don't want to get involved with this." I was a bit upset, but I understood his view and his opinion. He knew the risk and he knew the dangers. I respected what he had to say. So, without Bryan, we started to work with our own crew and equipment. Bruno Lemos and Kleber and myself started to think about and draw the idea of how that project could come about, but we needed money to produce this new idea. So we had to come up with some great strategies to make all this happen. Money is always needed for projects, unfortunately. That's just life.

One day before my wedding, I received a phone call from Garrett McNamara and he said, "Derek, can you jump on a plane and meet me in Nazaré?"

I said, "I would love to do it, but I'm getting married tomorrow and straight after we are going on a honeymoon to the Maldives and Thailand. It is all booked. There is no way I can cancel that. Also, my priority at the moment is to focus on my wedding and be married and enjoy our honeymoon so my wife and I can get to know each other. I'm sorry I can't make it, but definitely next time."

I was so glad that he understood and he encouraged me to focus on my wedding. Then he said, "Derek I'll be there for you next time. The winter surf season is finishing, but we can plan something right in the beginning of the next season, which will be in seven to eight months' time, and that will give you the ability to prepare yourself."

I was thinking on that day about the phone call I received from Garrett. My mind was ninety nine percent thinking about that for a few hours and only one percent on my wedding. My wife would not have been happy if she had known this at the time! I didn't mean to do that of course, but when you are presented with an opportunity to ride waves at Nazaré … well. But I knew that I had to fully focus on my wedding. It was going to be the happiest day in my life.

Natural disasters and fundraising

A few months later, I started to work really hard to improve my skills on big waves. We were training a lot and I also had to do some breath holding training to expand my lungs and to be able to hold my breath for as long as possible, as at Jaws and Nazaré, the hold down can be a long time. It can kill you and it has taken the lives of others. I wasn't ready to have my life ended at that time. There was far too much to accomplish and I had a new bride.

After training for a few months, the season for Jaws and Nazaré was coming up. The crew and I had to think how finances could be raised for me to get to those places. We had to become very creative. It would be quite an expensive trip to do, so the idea to do a fundraiser came up. My wife worked really hard on it. We launched the fundraiser and started to share with friends and people all over the world. It was an amazing opportunity. However, at the same time some natural phenomenas occurred. An earthquake in Mexico and a hurricane in Mexico and the Caribbean islands meant the whole world was working towards helping people who were affected by those events, bringing food and clothing to them. At the same time, I was doing a fundraiser to raise some money to go get some waves. It didn't seem right.

Maddy explained, "During that year, Derek was doing a lot of training. Then we went to Portugal to Nazaré. We started a fundraiser to make a movie about Derek chasing big waves. We raised $7,000, but that was only enough money to go to Portugal and surf with Garrett at Nazaré. The plan was to go to Portugal first and do Nazaré and then Hawaii to do Jaws, then Tahiti."

Of course it made me feel so bad. I felt selfish for a while, but I started to understand that God was in control and he would provide whatever he thought we would need. He did. We were able to raise a few thousand dollars, which was barely enough to take us to those places, but at least we were able to get there and start our movie. Finally, my dream was coming true.

After that, we got together and I travelled to Hawaii and we were prepared to surf at Jaws in Hawaii. One day I was surfing on the North Shore of Oahu just for training and I was riding some big, heavy waves over a reef. It was around sunset time and somehow I was not too confident. I was not relying on God; my mind was somewhere else. I was too worried about a number of things. I was getting this wave and somehow I fell off my surfboard. I got so pounded and the pressure of the wave took me deeper and deeper until I hit the rocks. It was the worst hold down I have ever had in big waves. I started to panic. I had to inflate my vest and finally that took me up and I could breathe again. So the ski came and rescued me and I told Garrett, "Hey, I think I'm done for the day." That really shook me up, but it was a big lesson I learnt: to keep focused on what I had to do and rely on God.

Jaws or God's Rock?

One or two days later, we flew to Maui where Jaws was breaking and it was a beautiful afternoon. We went on the harbor. It was not going to be Garrett towing me in at Jaws, but he did give me great advice. He recommended a great driver to tow me. We went out there that evening. I was so nervous I could barely ski on the rope. It was also very bumpy and that made it so difficult for me. So we tried for an hour or so, but we all realized it was not going to be the best moment.

We decided to wait for the next swell, which was going to show up in the next few days according to the weather forecast. We got all the skis and the drivers and we organized a boat to be out there if we needed extra help. So everything was going to be perfect and then when we woke up the next day. The forecast didn't confirm the weather was going to be as good as was initially promised. The wind was blowing very strong in the wrong direction and the swell didn't pick up that much. That was in the morning and we checked the forecast for the afternoon and they said it was supposed to get even worse.

At the same time, Garrett was texting us videos of the waves in front of his house from 'God's Rock' in Oahu. It was absolutely perfect – around 30 feet – glassy and beautiful. He was filming live on a video call on his ski. Garrett said, "I wish you were here, it would be perfect for you. Jaws is not going to break good today."

I just love the way Garrett is, with a lot of energy and so much enthusiasm. Obviously I could not see, but the team with me was telling me what it looked like. All together we made a decision to fly the whole crew back to Oahu, which is only half an hour flight, but getting to Garrett's house would take us three hours to get there and be ready for surfing. This is what crazy surfers do – anything to get great waves!

Then we started to get ready and Garrett and all of us double-checked the forecast for Oahu to make sure it would still be good in the afternoon. We all saw that the forecast was just confirming: it was going to get better and better. No wind at all in the afternoon – just better conditions at God's Rock, so we flew over and landed at Oahu. While the plane was landing, Bruno looked at me and said, "It looks so windy here I can see the bumps."

I said, "Don't even say that." I didn't want to hear anything negative about the waves. We got to the airport then drove to Garrett's house and when we got there and walked towards the ocean, we all almost had a heart attack. We couldn't even think – we were so mind blown when we looked at the waves. It was absolutely terrible. The wind was blowing so strong; it was white wash everywhere. The waves were closing out. It was truly impossible for surfing; the conditions were definitely very bad. We were speechless, but we had at least tried and we knew that Jaws was also bad for surfing.

What a dilemma we were in. It was already afternoon time around 4p.m. so a friend of ours from Maui called us and then he told us that everything changed over there in Maui. The waves were perfect. It was not the way the forecast had predicted. They had made a mistake again, but this time the surf was good for Jaws. Then we were so disappointed. We regretted that we came back to Oahu, regretted we didn't stay. But I said, "Let's not regret, let's be grateful we did it. Can you image what would have happened. We at least tried. We were brave; we did our best to make it happen. It's just not time yet." I was trying to be positive for everyone. You cannot live your life with regrets, only live with gratitude.

In life, we need to understand it's not always in our time. Certain things need to happen the way it is written in our destiny and we need to follow the path and be ready to climb step by step. We hung out in Oahu for a few more days, then finally we flew back to Jaws in Maui. This time we were so positive. We knew I was going to get some good waves. Once again we prepared everything – the same logistics with the skis and boat. I was honestly not too nervous, but I was making a few mistakes and I was not sure why. I was often falling off the surfboard right after the take off, but after a while, I could make it. I finally rode some waves at the mysterious Jaws.

Jaws is a really scary name for a wave, but it's definitely something unreal. The name really explains the phenomena of those waves. There is a cliff that is so hard to climb down and you have to go over some rocks to get into the water. When the wave breaks, it's a really interesting noise that it makes. It's a huge right hand barrel, which is very steep, breaking towards the channel. There is also a perfect left hand wave that breaks in an amazing shape.

When I was surfing the left hand waves, I was so amazed. The waves were around 25 to 30 feet and I felt like I had accomplished something great. I felt like a child with its favorite toy. Don't ask me how to explain this feeling; it's something that just sets my adrenaline soaring.

I rode a lot of waves on that day, but something was still stirring in my heart. I had the feeling I wanted to go bigger and bigger, so after I was done with surfing, the crew who were filming me and rescuing me had a chance to get some waves as well. I had this little Go-Pro in my hand that the pilot who was doing the rescue gave me. He knew I was going to be on the back of the rescue ski and he asked me, "When the driver is doing the rescue, he will also be driving the ski along the wave when I'm surfing."

I said, "Cool."

He said, "Just point this Go-Pro towards the wave and then you can film me."

I said, "Yes, I will do it." I was excited to do it. It's always a nice feeling to be on the ski and to be driven around when the waves are breaking. So after he got his first wave, when the ski was going through the waves, somehow I fell off and the wave took me under and I lost the Go-Pro that was in my hands. But until that moment, everything had gone smoothly. We got back to the boat, but then we realized that the Go-Pro was the same one that was on my surfboard when I was surfing, so all the footage that was taken was lost. That was such a shame and we were all so mad. Obviously we had the other angles with different cameras, but that specific footage from close to my surfboard was unique and it was really bad to lose it.

All was not lost

I couldn't believe I lost that camera. The emotions I felt cannot be explained. I had photographed so much surfing and was so excited I had captured all of this... and then to lose it all. I was totally devastated, *How could I have done this? I have lost everything*, I asked myself over and over. I really felt like sitting down and crying for a short time, but I didn't and I did not allow that to put me down. I was feeling so blessed and accomplished at what I had achieved. When all was said and done, I had so much fun and we had a great time in Maui.

Being on the ski is a good way for me to feel and sense how the waves are breaking – how the movements of the water are going. I can feel the wind, and not only do I rely on the adrenaline, but a set of facts coming together that helps me to decide in my mind how the moment feels. So that's why I like to be on the back of the ski. It is such a wonderful feeling and I feel very much in control. I was excited because I knew there was something else coming up. My dream to be a big wave rider would not stop with just one surf session. That would be something I wanted to do and carry with me my whole life.

I received some emails from a really well known big wave rider telling me that he knows that I have a lot of skills, but also telling me that I should stop doing what I was doing, that I should not even think anymore about surfing Nazaré. That I had no idea how dangerous Nazaré was and I was putting myself at risk, as well as my family and friends. I felt very discouraged. I felt like I was stupid and I was doing something for no reason at all and I was being very selfish. But that was not true. No one understood what was going on in my mind. No one understood how strong my desires were and that I never wanted to prove anything to anyone – not even to myself. I just wanted to do what I always dreamt about, which was to ride big waves and my goal was to get a wave at Nazaré. That was my dream and I was determined that I wouldn't let anything or anyone stop me from achieving this.

It's very hard to understand someone when that person has a really strong view on a matter. You are driven by your thoughts and what you are willing to do. In my mind, I was all about taking off on a humungous wave at Nazaré – something gigantic. When someone is on that level of desiring things so badly, there is a flame inside you that keeps burning, but the fuel never ends. That's how I've been my whole life and that's how I want to be because it makes me strong and it inspires people to be happy and to set their goals and accomplish their dreams.

Nazaré part one
The time to go to Nazaré was getting closer and I was getting very nervous, but really excited at the same time, so we finally flew to Portugal, which is one of my favorite countries to be in. I love the culture, I love the people. The waves are really good and the food is absolutely delicious.
Bruno Lemos and Kleber were with me, but unfortunately my wife had not arrived. She was busy with her work at that time in Germany. She would only be able to come the following week. I was not too comfortable that my wife was not there with me, especially because she encourages me a lot. She calms me down. We pray together and I was missing her.

Garrett was also there and he was really thrilled to tow me, but the first few days when I got there, the waves were not too big. They were only around six to eight feet, really only for paddling. I got my surfboard and I paddled out with a friend of mine. I was so confident, as a few years before, I had a great time at Nazaré surfing some head-high waves with my friend, Magno. I had so much fun and I got some great barrels. I already knew how powerful the waves were, even when they were small. I was ready to have some fun just paddling with my mates. That was all we could do when there were no giant swells where you could do towing.

MY DESTINY – NAZARÉ AND JAWS

When I got on the outside, a set of waves came and we were paddling over to get through and my friend told me, "Just duck dive." He was a couple of meters in front me. We duck dived under the wave. He made it through, but unfortunately I didn't. The wave closed out right on me. It felt like I was inside a washing machine, churning and churning. I got dragged all the way to the sand. I thought, *If this can happen in small waves, what can happen in the big waves?* I was trying to imagine what would have happened if the same thing happened on a big day. That was an interesting situation, but at the same moment it made me a little terrified. *Was I doing the right thing?* I wondered.

In a few days we knew there was going to be some swell coming. We got together everything we needed to be out there in the ocean. We woke up one morning and the waves were great, but it was so foggy and my team and I were wondering about the fog. I said, "Hey I don't care, I'm blind. I surf by feeling."

But Garrett and our friends said, "But we can't see and film it. We want to register that moment." We had to wait for the fog to go away and I was so anxious that I couldn't wait. I didn't have my wife over there with me and I felt lonely. I really missed her. I called her and asked her to pray with me over the phone, as I was about to get the biggest wave of my life.

She prayed and she encouraged me, as I was so nervous. I guess reality was setting in. Straight after the fog cleared, we got ready to jump on the skis and drive to the waves. When we got there, it was a little weird. Some surfers could not understand why I was there and some of them even said it was very dangerous for me, as the waves were quite big. I listened to them and respected what they said, but we still did our own thing. Nothing would stop me.

Finally, a wave came towards me and Garrett got ready to tow me in. When I was about to catch this wave, I felt quite nervous, but I was also praying to God to protect me. Then I got the wave and I rode it for a little bit. It was extremely powerful and strong, so I finished riding the wave. Then the ski came and got me and I was excited. I was thinking all the time that I was so grateful I didn't have any injuries. It was such a feeling of exuberance.

Actually, to be honest, that wave was not too big. I had the feeling of accomplishment because I did get a wave in Nazaré and that was my goal, but I knew there was something missing because I didn't get the really big wave that I was looking for. There was still more to be achieved.

We all went back to the house where we were staying and Bruno and Kleber were taking a look at the footage they had filmed for the movie we were making. They said I did so well, but we needed something bigger. It didn't look like Nazaré. What more could I do? However, I knew they were right. I was already feeling like that, but we had to wait for the next swell to come up, which was actually good. It gave me time so Maddy could arrive and be with me. This was what I really wanted and needed – to have my wife by my side. She was such a calming and stable influence for me.

Nazaré part two

When Maddy arrived, I went to pick her up at the airport. I was so glad and happy to see her. I could feel her smile and it was so great to hug her. I was another person because we love each other so much and we love being together. She was my greatest support. So the day finally arrived and there we were, waiting for the next swell. Maddy was with me and all was well. We checked the forecast and knew something huge was going to come. I was already so nervous just thinking about what was going to descend upon me. I knew it was going to be big... in fact, huge! The day before, I was trying to concentrate on this momentous day. I was bringing all my focus onto the wave of my life.

It was really hard for me to sleep the night before. I was rolling around on my bed because I was thinking too much. Then finally the next day arrived and we were getting dressed at the house where the harbor is. I not only had to wear my inflatable vest, but also a very thick suit, as it is really cold in Nazaré. That suit has a lot of pads and it gives you more flotation if the waves smash you. I was well prepared.

Then we got on our skis and we drove out of the harbor. When we got outside of Nazaré, I asked Garrett to stop the ski because I wanted to say a prayer. This was vitally important to me. I prayed and I felt the presence of God upon our lives. It was so awesome to be connected to God. It was a great experience because the sky was very cloudy and after the prayer, I could feel the sun shining down on me. Garrett said, "Derek, your payers are so powerful. The sky is blue, the sun is out and the waves are perfect."

I was so confident then. Sometimes when I go surfing, the waves are not that big, yet I don't have that confidence in me. So this time we got out in the ocean and I let Garrett get some waves. There were some other surfers there and Garrett managed to get some good waves. After, it was my time. I jumped in the water, got the surfboard, got on the ski, I put my feet in, I grabbed the rope and Garrett started to drive me towards the wave. We had a command that we use when I need to let the rope go. They say, "Vai, vai," and I know then to let the rope go. Then the adrenalin starts!

So when Garrett said, "Vai," my heart was pumping and I did this amazing take off on this beautiful left hand wave. I went all the way down the line. I had so much speed on my surfboard that I kept going. I rode the wave for a while; it was a fairly long ride. Normally the challenge at Nazaré is to finish riding the waves at the right moment. You don't want to end the wave on the bottom, otherwise you'll get 'smoked' by the waves. What you do there is you ride as much as you can and you get out of the wave through the top, so this way the ski also has time to rescue you before another wave comes.

That was going to be my biggest challenge because it's really hard for me to figure out where is the right spot to get out. What amazed me and everyone else about the wave I rode is that I did it so perfectly. I rode so nicely and I got out through the top. When I finished riding, after Garrett got me on the ski, he was screaming because he was so happy to see what happened and also everyone else out there surfing was clapping and cheering for me because they were amazed at how good I rode the wave. I was so happy about that. It gave me so much confidence. I was absolutely astonished at what I had accomplished.

I am basically sharing what people were saying about that wave because they could not believe I was blind as I rode that wave so perfectly. They said there were actually two surfers on the wave and only a short space between and I went perfectly through. I was on my own, just appreciating the truth that I was not surfing that wave by myself. God was leading me with his hand. I was able to share that with people and bring honor and glory to God.

Then we got out of the water and I was listening to what people were talking about. The whole town of Nazaré was commenting about the blind surfer's wave that he got that day. I felt so accomplished and grateful to every single person who helped me directly or indirectly, either in Nazaré, or our fundraising, by prayers, by encouragement.

The wave that I got on that day was around 25 to 30 feet, pretty much the same size as I got at Jaws. I knew there were going to be some more waves the next day, but I also knew that Garrett wanted to surf himself, as he was focused on me only for a long time. It surprised me when Garrett came to me that night and said, "Hey Derek, be ready for tomorrow. I'm going to tow you into a 'bomb'. Tomorrow is your day."

I was thinking to myself, *What is he talking about?* I already got the great wave today. But I said, "Sounds good. I will be stoked tomorrow to get some more waves." But what was coming?

Bryan Jennings said, "Derek knew there was more. There was still something in his heart. He wanted to surf the biggest wave in the world. He was striving for the big wave. He was encouraged by all the people he met, but he knew that wasn't the wave he wanted to surf."

That evening, I was actually very chilled and relaxed, as was Maddy, but it was still hard to sleep that night because I knew I was going to surf again the next day. I woke up very nervous because from my bedroom, I could already hear the waves crashing. Then I could tell that the waves were actually much bigger than yesterday. Then I said to myself, *Derek, you are already there, now keep going. You can't give up.* The only thing that could hold me back and not allow me to achieve my dream was myself. Today was the one chance in my life to get a gigantic wave. This is what I had wanted to do for so many years. I could not even eat breakfast, as I was so nervous. All I had was a glass of water and fresh squeezed orange juice.

The monster

Maddy said, "When finally the day arrived that Derek was going to surf the monster, I was really nervous. He said, 'Honey I am nervous.' So I was nervous because he was nervous."

Once again, we all met at the harbor and got ready. All the equipment was there. I was touching up the surfboard I was going to use again. It's a really heavy surfboard because when you do tow-in surf, you want to use a heavy board according to the surf conditions. The more bumps and the bigger the waves are, the heavier the board should be so it can hold the pressure. I was riding a six-foot long tow surfboard with 26 pounds on it.

Then we got all we needed on the ski. I had my suit on and the guys with the cameras were there. I had my wife sitting on the cliff cheering and praying for me and I had God with his hands upon my life. Somehow, I knew there was going to be something special that morning.

We drove to the ocean through the harbor. Garrett let me drive the ski for a short time so I could chill out a bit. Driving the ski is something I love to do – it gives me freedom. It's so much fun for me. We stayed there for about 2 ½ hours trying to choose a perfect wave. The waves were solid, heavy 40 to 50 foot waves. In other words, mountains! I knew where I was going to put myself. The game was getting more serious. *What was I letting myself in for?* I thought to myself.

Before I got any waves, Garrett drove me to the outside so I could feel the power of the waves breaking and the movement of the water. I could taste the salt water on my lips. I started to pray for protection and wisdom and for God's will to be done in my life. I mean this was serious stuff. Right after that prayer, everything changed. I was another person. I was not nervous anymore. I was so confident like never before. I knew that my time over there for this great wave was coming. Then Garrett said, "Derek, get ready, here you go. I'm going to get you a bomb." Then he started to drive the jet ski and I was holding on to the rope on the surfboard and he said, "Derek, it's the perfect wave, the one you always dreamt about your whole life. It's perfect, do your best." In that same moment, I started to sing a worship song to God. I began to sing the song 'Oceans' and I started to feel such a peace in my heart and a strong presence of God around me.

When Garrett said, "Vai," I let go of the rope and I started to begin to descend that giant mountain. When I was right on the top at the beginning of the take off, I could feel that that wave was going to be something very different to anything else I had ridden. I had just so much speed on my surfboard. It felt like I was going down the mountain on a snowboard run. There were many bumps that tried to cause me to fall, but I kept putting a lot of pressure on my foot and I could hold on to it. The take off all the way down to the line was super long and so fast, but I made it all the way down. Even though it was so fast and so long, with a lot of speed, everything felt for me like it was slow motion.

I could live every second of that wave and every second for me felt like it was one minute. Because I was so 'in the moment' and it was so intense, I was trying to appreciate it as much as I could. It felt like my heart was jumping; it felt like there was a party going on inside of my heart. I finished my wave, but unfortunately I couldn't make it through the top because it closed out. When I fell off the surfboard, I could hear that monster mountain falling over me. I thought to myself, *Now I am in trouble.*

A huge bump appeared on the wave causing me to fall off my board. I could not hold my balance. There was too much speed and bumps at the same time. When you can see, you can prepare yourself for the wipeout that is to come, but as I cannot see, they always surprise me, so I never know when it is going to happen.

I was under the water, trying to deal with the hold down and getting pounded. It was so very frightening. Finally, I came up to the surface and I could take a breath and I thought the ski would be there to rescue me. Unfortunately, as the hold down on the previous wave was so long, when I came up, the second wave was right on me already. So I had to deal with getting pounded again. Could I handle this?

The second huge wave from the set swamped me and I had no idea where the wave was coming from because it was so hard to hear it.

There was a lot of whitewater moving around, so I could not figure out which way was the shore and which way was the outside so I could at least duck under the wave when it was about to break. That wave just literally pounded me down so bad that I had to inflate my life vest, otherwise I would not be able to survive the long time under the water. I was very scared; I thought this was the end of me. It is such a horrible and frightening feeling to be held under the water trying to hold your breath, not knowing if you would ever make it to the surface and survive. Of course, it's even worse when you can't see anything. The fear of drowning is a real thing for a big wave surfer.

Finally, I came up and then the ski was coming to rescue me, but they had a short time to get me because a third wave was coming. That was frightening, as I wasn't sure I could handle another attack. When the ski was approaching me, I had to hold on to the handles. I missed it because it came by so fast, as there was another wave coming. So in a short time, I had to prepare myself to get pounded once more. I wasn't sure at that stage if I would survive. That's the time when you call out to God and you really, really need Him.

The third wave was not as big as the first two, but I did stay under the water for a little while. I had to inflate my vest again so I could come up to the surface. I was feeling so very nervous when I was pounded by the third wave. I was lost underneath that monster that was trying to take my life. I was being churned in every way. I thought this was the end of me. It was a terrifying ordeal.

Finally, the set was gone and I thought to myself, *To get one huge wave in life, you have to get pounded three times after. That is bad.* But I was so excited, so happy and so elated. I was celebrating like I had never celebrated before.

After that, everyone came to me to congratulate me and all the surfers in the water were clapping again, much more than the day before. They were saying out loud, "Derek, that was awesome. Congratulations, you got the wave of the day." Many of them were telling me, "You're the rider of the year." After we came out of the water, everyone was hugging me. It was funny because I felt like I was a hero, but I'm not. The feeling of accomplishment is something unreal – something I carry around with me all the time.

Maddy explained, "That day of the big wave, I was sitting on a high hill. I was with Bruno and he was filming and others were filming from everywhere. I had to wait two hours until Derek finally got on a wave. I had to keep looking to see if it was Derek. Fortunately, we had a walkie-talkie, which helped us communicate with Garrett.

"Riding that big wave, it was amazing how long he was able to stay on it, but then he was smashed by it. For me, it was a bit scary. I was looking to find his head, waiting for him to come up and praying, 'God protect him.' Then another two waves came before they could rescue him. So he was smashed another two times. The jet ski came in to rescue him, but they couldn't make it, so they had to wait to the side while he was pounded underwater. In the end, he was fine. We were all thinking he would be terrible. Then Garrett was on the line telling us Derek had just asked him if he could do another one. Luckily, Garrett didn't agree to this. Incredibly, there was no injury to Derek – he was perfect. So I could breathe again after that. I'm glad I could be there. It was so amazing what Derek did. I was so proud of him.

Bruno said, "Derek still wants to ride big waves. He wants bigger and bigger, until there is nothing that is bigger. But I don't want to see Derek on anything bigger.' When I told Derek this, he got angry and said,

'I can do bigger and bigger.' Derek is very determined. He always wants better and larger. He doesn't know when to stop and I don't think he ever will stop unless there was a physical problem. The wave in Nazaré is the biggest in the world. Derek rode this, but there is even greater and he wants to ride this. He wants to break a record. He has already broken a record – a blind man riding the biggest wave in the world!

"I was out there with Derek in Nazaré, Portugal to ride the biggest wave. I wasn't on the ski; I was on the cliff next to Maddy. I was photographing Derek riding the waves from the cliff. My first thoughts were he was going to die riding that huge wave and the rescue was really hard. I thought he was in trouble, but he did really well. However, I was scared for him. It was something – just a weird feeling I had. I was happy because he got to the bottom of the wave, but I was also scared because he got wiped out.

"I was really impressed by Derek and so much in awe of him in how he was able to negotiate those monsters. We showed the picture to some people who surf big waves and they were in awe of what Derek had accomplished.

"He has already achieved something beyond great. Something no one has ever thought about. I think he feels like he has failed because he said he wants more. Because he didn't complete the wave 100 per cent, he thought he had failed. But no one else has thought this. He made the hardest part – the drop. I was just so proud of him."

I'm so grateful that my father always encouraged me to do anything I want, even when I told him I wanted to surf Nazaré. He talked to me about the risks I would have to encounter and how dangerous it was, but he still supported me and encouraged me to do it.

I'm glad I had many friends praying for me and also my wife, my mother and my grandmother. Those three amazing women were constantly together in their prayers. Being able to surf those giant waves just gave me many more chances to inspire people, to show people we can do anything in life, no matter if we are blind or if we have any other challenges or problems. It's just the fact of eliminating the negative thoughts and starting to feed ourselves with good and positive thoughts with belief and also faith.

In life, we have to make decisions – no matter what it will be. We cannot be double-minded and not knowing what to do. We have to choose one way to go. We have to make a choice. When we make a choice, at the end of the day, even if we made the wrong choice, at least we made a decision. For me, it's better to regret after making a decision than to not make any at all. For example, we were in Jaws and the waves were really good in Oahu. We went to Oahu and the waves were really, really bad. I did not regret that we went to Oahu because I don't like to live in regret. It would have been much worse if I had not made the decision of going to Oahu and stayed at Jaws. Then imagine if the waves were really good in Oahu. That's life – you step out and do something.

Many people were always asking me, "Why do you want to ride big waves? It really is unnecessary to do it." Friends and people I didn't know would also come to me and say that it was so dangerous to ride those waves, I had no idea what I was doing and I should stop. They would say there was no reason to do this and I didn't have to prove anything else to the world. I have already done so much and it wasn't worth continuing, as I was putting myself at risk. This is what was being presented to me constantly.

However, they didn't understand about dreams and about pursing and accomplishing what is in your heart. They had no idea what a strong desire in your heart can make you do. Also, many people don't know where a strong faith in God can take you. With trust in God, you can do anything.

Nothing is impossible.

EPILOGUE

This is the journey of my step into a life with Jesus Christ, a life I would not have missed for anything. I am so honored and blessed to have met Almighty God. I don't know where my life would have ended up if he hadn't reached out and saved me. My gratitude is beyond words. May my life continue to bring honor to Him.

I was born into a Christian family. I went to church because my mother and grandmother and father took me. I didn't go on my own resolution. When I was a teenager, about 15 years old, I realized I needed to make that decision on my own – my own choice. I knew that there was something missing in my life. I was not complete. Then I started to go to church because it was what I wanted, not someone else.

There were many years of ups and downs. I was near and far from God, and I believe I was never actually really committed to God because if I was, then I wouldn't have been far from him. Since then, I have become stronger and stronger with my relationship with God. This is how I have overcome my difficulties and achieved what has been given to me for my destiny.

I had the wonderful honour of carrying the Olympic Torch in Brazil. My manager called me while I was in Australia to say I had the opportunity to carry the torch. I thought, *I'm sure they won't have a surfer doing this*. Six months after I received an email from the Olympic Committee saying that I was selected to carry the torch. I couldn't believe it. In my city, there were at least two or three Olympic athletes. When I told my mother and father the news, everyone in our city was saying, "Someone else will carry the torch, not you."

I was unsure because I had the email. It was true: I did carry the torch! It was an amazing experience, particularly doing it in my home town. I was the first athlete to carry the torch near the ocean. It was like recognition of how much I had to overcome. This was an unbelievable experience – they chose me! The fact I carried the torch represented all of the water sports in the Olympics because the torch goes around the country into every single city.

My life so far seems to have been a whirlwind: constant traveling, overcoming, stepping out in faith and trusting Almighty God. But I have had some wonderful experiences.

So after getting married, Maddy and I traveled quite a bit for at least a year. We were not based anywhere; we had nowhere to call home. Even though we really enjoyed traveling and getting to know new places and being well received into people's homes, we always wanted to have our own place. We wanted to have a place that we could always come back to. Traveling after marriage was amazing and people would always make us feel at home, but we still had the desire to have a home.

So we had finally settled in San Clemente in California and we were becoming so comfortable there, but unfortunately our time was getting closer to the end of living in America. When we realized we were going to move away and a new journey was about to start, we understood that it would be a huge impact on our minds and our lives. When we realized that we were going to move away from America, I was asking God why he brought us to America just for 18 months. Why would He do it? Maddy was really upset because she had made friends, she found a nice church and she made our home look so nice and pretty, and then we had to get rid of everything.

I started to get a little depressed. I could barely think about anything else – only the move and where we were going. One day, Maddy and I were together and said, "You know what: we've got to be happy, whatever the future holds for us and whatever God is bringing to us. Let's be happy with the new journey and pray to God as to where to go."

Then we started to pack everything up, but we had made that important decision to be happy and not to complain and be grateful for the time we spent in San Clemente. We were thankful for the great things that had happened and the great things we had done. When we started to think like that, things changed. We were getting ready for a new life, even though we didn't know yet where we were going to go.

Our time was getting closer to the end of our journey in America. Maddy had decided to spend some time with my family in Brazil and her family in Germany. In the meantime, we were praying and hearing from God where he wanted us to go. Our own plan was to end up living in Portugal, but we were willing to go wherever God wants to take us.

However, after a while I did not feel any peace about going to Portugal, even though it's something Maddy and I really wanted to do. It's perfect as it is close to Maddy's family in Germany and close to my family in Brazil. So we decided to go to Brazil for now, spend a little time over there and try to hear from God as to where He wants us.

I have some new opportunities in South Brazil. That's why I made the decision to stay in Brazil. I am already a motivational speaker and I am getting myself prepared so I can get to a high level of my speech to everyone. I'm doing some courses and training and really recognizing people who are great in marketing. I also feel other doors are starting to open in Brazil. A TV channel, the biggest in Brazil, wants to do a series with me featuring me riding big waves in different spots, so we will go to places to film big waves.

My goal is to do motivational speaking all around the world. I want to help people and encourage them to go beyond their limits. I want to show people to break their fear down. I want to tell people that we should be controlling our fear, not fear controlling us. I want to tell people they can do anything and overcome any single difficult they have had – that they can do the impossible. I want to use my story to help people.

Anyone who wants to step out into the unknown must do so with faith in their God, be fearless and have tenacity. For me, to have achieved all that I have done has taken all of the above. It hasn't always been easy – in fact it has often been a huge struggle – but I was relentless, so relentless that some might call it reckless.

To have come this far in life and achieved all that I have done is also due to my loving family and friends. Everyone needs this great support. There have been many people who have impacted my life, some in major ways and some in more minor ways, but all have been significant.

I have definitely developed in my character. I have become more fearless, more tenacious and more trusting in my Heavenly Father. I have learnt so much. Life is a journey, full of surprises and adventures. So, my life is taking off again into new dimensions, but I am so excited about my destiny.

I want to say to all who read this book and who listen to my story and see my videos: if I can do all this and I'm blind, what can you do? I encourage you to step out in faith and live life to the fullest.

I want to thank you for reading my book and I invite you to become powerful forces for good and angels on the planet.

Derek Rabelo

TESTIMONIALS

ADAM HANSEN *Personal trainer and friend*

Derek Rabelo. Well, what can I say about him that's probably not already been said? He is one of the most inspiring guys I have ever met.

When Derek was in Perth in Western Australia, I met him at the gym where I was working. He came in to work out and we instantly connected. Then I started to do some training with him. We also ended up surfing together, as we had a common bond with that sport. When I was with Derek for the first time in the ocean, I was blown away by his surfing ability. I absolutely couldn't believe it at first; he handled himself so well in the water.

What I see in Derek is that he seems to be fearless. He has minimal concern for the consequences of what could happen – not just in the water, but anywhere because he has a deep faith in God and that he is looking after him. His belief seems to permeate into every single cell of his body. That's my feeling, that's how I perceive him.

Derek has an unbelievable sense of being able to accomplish whatever is before him. He can do some things even better than people with sight. Everything is heightened. His sense of smell and intuition is phenomenal. He can register things about people that normally you would only get if who can see. Derek can have an understanding of what a person looks like, such as if they are overweight or skinny. It is unbelievable.

We see his limitations of being blind, but Derek makes you realize that this is definitely not the case for him. He helps to show people that there are no obstacles and you can tackle anything, no matter what. Most of us would think the world is against us if we had a disability. We would think 'poor me,' but Derek thinks about the next adventure – what's the next extreme activity he can try? I call him a massive adrenalin junkie.

I think Derek is crazy surfing big waves. I've been surfing since I was 12 years old and there is no way I would do that. I think it may be because he can't see what is coming. That's what I tell him, I say, "Derek, if you saw the wave coming towards you, then… "

When you first meet Derek you are on a high being in his presence and other people experience this as well. He creates a high frequency around him because of his energy.

BRYAN JENNINGS *Movie Producer*

Derek has really inspired and motivated me. Derek has taught me what it means to live by faith and not by sight. Everything he does is by faith and with great courage. He does not give himself excuses to avoid any challenges that come his way, so why would we give ourselves excuses if Derek doesn't?

I met Derek Rabelo when I was showing the movie we made together, 'Walking On Water,' in Rio, Brazil. The following day we all went surfing together and when I watched Derek paddle out by himself and catch a few waves, I was so inspired that I knew I needed to produce his documentary and share his story with the world.

The one thing that stands out about Derek is that he is a troublemaker (in a good way) and makes everyone laugh. He has a huge heart and loves all people and that love is so evident in his life.

Derek has a dependency upon God that we all should have and his faith has aided him to achieve all he has done as a blind person. How does he accomplish surfing? many people would ask? He knows that God will protect him and bless him because he has seen it happen so often.

Derek inspires and motivates all people who meet him and know of him. Producing the 'Beyond Sight' movie with Derek, teaching him English and traveling all over the world together has been so special. We have laughed together, shared our faith with hundreds of thousands of people, surfed many surf spots together, and we have become very close friends. I am so thankful for Derek in my life.

One favourite memory was when we did a movie and showed it in San Diego for 300 homeless people. The theater smelled terrible, but as we walked out, Derek told me it was his favorite movie screening we had done because he knew the homeless people were special and that God had blessed them that day. It just shows Derek's heart for people who are in difficult situations.

When I saw the photo of Derek surfing a huge wave at Nazaré in Portugal, it was probably one of the most amazing things I have seen in my life. I can't believe the surf industry didn't make something of this. They should have put him on the cover of every magazine in the world. It is similar to the blind person who climbed Mount Everest.

BRUNO LEMOS *Movie Producer and Filmographer*

The first time I met Derek, we were at church in Hawaii. His friend, Magno, brought him along. Magno introduced me to him, but didn't say he was blind. Then Magno said, "He's blind and he's going to surf

Pipeline." I thought it was a joke. Then I realized this was serious stuff, so I decided to film Derek surfing. We did a short video and people were amazed.

My first thought was to do a film to showcase him at the Maui Film Festival. Then the story became so fascinating to me. I had been working in the surfing industry for over 20 years, but this story was beyond our surfing world.

Once we started to film this documentary, we could see God's hands moving. Every person we contacted, everything we tried to do that was important God was already helping us.

When I sat Derek down for an interview, the first thing I sensed was the story was incredible. It was utterly amazing. Then I called up a friend who works in a TV station in Honolulo, Luiz, because he had experience with documentaries and production. I told him we have this amazing account here of Derek's life. I think we have a very good story for a documentary. That's what I conveyed to him. Hence the movie was made.

I see a lot of perseverance in Derek. He also has a strong faith in God. His mom has a lot to do with that. She was the one who was praying since day one when she knew Derek was blind. She raised him in the way Derek got to know the Lord. We are really close friends with her. She prays a lot for Derek. Derek's mother has had a big role in his spiritual life.

Also, I believe, the gift that Derek has to surf… well, it's not normal. No one in the surfing industry has seen or heard a story like this. It is the most incredible story we surfers have ever heard. We could see that whenever a legend of the surf met Derek, they would be baffled. They were at a loss to understand how a blind man could surf such big waves.

Derek inspires even those who motivate others. He is a huge source of inspiration, especially in the surfing world. When you don't surf, you don't comprehend the ramifications of the huge waves that any surfer has to battle, let alone someone who cannot see what is crashing down upon him.

God definitely had a purpose for Derek. I was one of the first guys pushing Derek to write a book.

CHRISTIAN McCUDDEN *Senior Pastor, C3 Noosa*

Where do you start with Derek? Derek possesses so many great attributes and is one of the most inspiring individuals I have ever had the pleasure of meeting. Derek's positive attitude towards life and his faith in God stand out to me as being two of his greatest attributes.

I invited Derek to our church – C3 Noosa in Queensland, Australia - as I wanted to encourage our people through Derek's life and story that not only is nothing impossible, but that our perceived setbacks can often become our greatest strengths in life when viewed and channeled the right way.

As expected, Watching Derek's video of him downhill speed skating blew everyone's mind!

Derek is very inspiring to me personally. I may be able to see naturally, but he has an amazing ability to dream and as he steps out into those dreams, he creates a life, which very few able-bodied and sight seeing individuals achieve.

I think Derek's faith is his greatest strength in life and his lack of sight has enabled him to work the faith muscle we all possess, but don't all use!

Everyone in life has their disability. Derek's is evident, but for others they can be hidden. I believe every person has to make a personal decision to look beyond and then push beyond whatever disability or limitation they have and by faith, embrace a life of dreaming and adventure.

If Derek can do it, you can also do it. Don't give up on your dreams; live passionately and let God into the most intimate parts of your world so that he can take you beyond what you've ever dreamt of doing.

GLENN WYSMAN *Senior Pastor, The Link*

Derek Rabelo is one inspirational guy. He inspires and motivates everyone he meets. I am so impressed at his tenacity in never giving up.

I came to know about Derek through a friend of his, Bryan Jennings, the producer of his new movie at that time, 'Beyond Sight'. We went to the premiere of that movie and met Derek there.

I was really inspired after seeing Derek's movie and meeting him. His story is extremely moving, to say the least. It was then that I believed it was a good fit to ask if Derek was able to speak at our church, which is The Link on the Northern Beaches of Sydney. I knew my congregation would really appreciate hearing his amazing and life-changing story.

Derek's story relates to people of all ages, as I believe we all at some point or points in our lives feel vulnerable and fearful of the unknown. His message 'Walk by faith, not by sight' takes on a whole new level when speaking with Derek and watching his movie. I don't think he could do all he is accomplishing without a strong faith and belief in God.

As a Pastor, meeting Derek a few times has always had an impact on me personally. It stirs my faith to press on and believe anything is possible. I would like to say that the journey of Derek Rabelo moved my congregation and me 100% - how couldn't it! You feel you have no excuses after hearing and seeing his journey.

Derek is a passionate and energised individual and has achieved many remarkable things. I believe his relationship with God has anchored him and kept his focus on the right path. God does indeed protect and he certainly has protected Derek on some of his wild adventures.

Not all of us would like to ride a big wave, or skate down a hill like Derek, but I do believe every human wants to live out their life with purpose. To accomplish what he has and stay the course to become an influence within his sphere and to inspire others around the world is so encouraging.

CJ HOPGOOD *Former professional surfer*

When I hang out or see Derek, my first thoughts are How weak I am? What little amount of faith I have. I actually wish I had as much faith as this guy. I really wish I was on this guy's level.

Derek was young when I first met him. He still has not lost that childlike quality you have to have in life. At that time when I first started surfing with Derek, I tried to keep my eyes closed and I imagined how I would be able to catch a wave if I was blind. It is the scariest thing in the world. How does this guy do it?

To me, to be in Derek's space, there is such great inspiration. It is something special - something that is hard to put into words. When I look at Derek, I can see his faith. When you meet him, you're trying to imagine everything that has happened in his life and what he is going through. Derek has to have an immense amount of faith to achieve his dreams... in fact just to get through life being blind. He has to ask God for everything. Derek is extremely smart. I watched him pick up English very quickly.

I surfed many times with Derek and I was getting to know him really well. I always call Derek 'De Rab' so he always knew who was speaking to him. My brother and I are twins and whenever we saw Derek, it didn't matter how far we were. He could pick out which one of us was talking. Once I was in a lobby of a hotel and I called out, "De Rab." Derek knew who was calling him and he yelled out, "That's you, CJ." He is so tuned into everything. It is hilarious and so awesome to see.

Another funny story I will relay was when we were in Australia on the Gold Coast we were surfing at Greenmount. The sun was going down it was dusk. As I was drifting down to Kirra beach I saw Derek in the ocean and there was no one else around. 'What was going on,' I thought. 'What is De Rab doing here?' I called out, "De Rab, where is your friend? I'll hang with you and surf and meet you on the beach." We surfed almost until dark. I said, "Dude I am freaking right out."

Derek said, "I am here with a friend, but she had to go back to Western Australia. Don't worry CJ, she knows I'm not looking at any of the girls!" I was worried about his safety and here was cracking a joke. Those experiences I will remember for the rest of my life.

Derek and I were surfing Pipeline in Hawaii and I thought I had killed him! It was pretty scary out there, but he was determined to paddle out. Out in the surf, I said to him, "I'll get you a good wave. Just turn around and go." But then straight after I told him to go, I thought, 'I just killed De Rab!' I had thought it was a good wave, however I was mistaken. Fortunately I didn't kill him!

Derek has got to be the most peaceful person in the ocean's 'impact zone.' I always imagine Derek being so at peace. It is a special gift. We haven't scratched the surface yet, but Derek lives in that every day.

It's cool just to see a person shining as much light on God with his own story. He doesn't have to say a word; he is a living, breathing person of love, hope and peace.

EDDIE ROTHMAN *Big Wave Surfer*

You know, at first I couldn't believe – and I didn't want to believe – that Derek Rabelo was blind. I just couldn't fathom how he could ride waves without being able to see. I was soon to know the truth.

I met Derek and his Brazilian friend, Magno, down on the beach in front of my house one day. I called out and asked them to stop by. They both told me they wanted to surf Pipe. My sons were also there at the time. They were living next door and came over to meet them. We got Derek a surfboard and my sons took him to Pipe to surf. Bruno Lemos, the photographer, was also with them. I also went and was blown away. I said to myself, This guy can really surf.

I was surfing out the back and the group who was with Derek would tell him which wave to catch. I could see the wave was closing in front of him. I was performing a 'cut back' and somehow he knew this. I questioned this. I was saying to myself, This guy's not blind.

Derek stayed at my house for a while and it was only then I realized he really was blind. He stayed downstairs in my home and he kept on amazing me with the stuff he could do. He would walk around outside. People also let him drive the golf cart. I also surfed with him and was amazed at what he could accomplish.

Hawaii is not an easy place to surf for anyone, particularly if you are blind. Derek got along well with all of us, including the locals. I couldn't believe that he was doing what he was doing. I mean, he was a great athlete and he was blind! He ain't stopping this – he's going all the way in my mind. I couldn't believe what he was accomplishing.

When the movie was made about him, at first the producers said they didn't want my sons and I in it, but Derek insisted, so we ended up being included. When he went to go and surf at Nazaré in Portugal, I didn't want to help him because I thought it was too dangerous. I didn't want to be responsible for anything going wrong. However, he proved any skeptics wrong. The waves were really big. He is amazing. More than 99 percent of people in the world haven't ridden waves like these.

Derek had his parents and friends to back him up. He didn't need anybody else. He was on his path already. It was so ingrained in him. I saw it coming – I just walked away. God already had him. He was doing what he was meant to do.

GARRETT MCNAMARA *Big Wave Surfer*

When I think of Derek Rabelo, it's pretty unimaginable what he's doing and so unbelievable. I am sometimes at a loss to understand how he survives these waves and what drives him to ride those monsters. I am so inspired by him.

Derek is truly inspiring and he believes everything is definitely possible. He really shows us all that you can overcome anything and everything. If a blind man can surf a 40-foot wave, then everything else is achievable.

I believe that Derek definitely is stirring the world. People can't help but be encouraged. I'm talking about every single person in the world. The challenges they think are impossible all are achievable after watching him.

Derek has developed great persistence and surrounds himself with people who believe in him and help guide him. This has been very important for him to achieve what he has. The first time I saw Derek surfing, he was on a giant wave, 20 to 30 feet high, right in front of my house in Hawaii. My thoughts were, I don't understand how he can do it. He rode it perfectly for 100 yards or longer for more than 30 seconds. I admit I was a little worried and concerned (or maybe very concerned) when the waves were crashing on him. I was worried for his safety. Then he did so well and I got excited, but there was still that ongoing concern.

Derek has taken some giant waves and fallen badly. The scariest situation for him is when a wave lands on him and he is not aware of what is happening and people have to come and rescue him. He wants to ride even bigger waves. Those waves don't appear real when you look at them - let alone riding them when you are blind.

Derek is up for any challenge, he wants to ride bikes and he drove my jet ski. He drove me around on a pushbike in Hawaii. It was a bit scary, to say the least, but we made it. He takes things in his stride. I've witnessed some crazy things happening.

The mind is really powerful. Derek has a strong mind, strong will and strong faith as well. All this keeps him achieving the seemingly impossible. He definitely couldn't do all this without these strengths.

JEANINE TREHARNE – *Co Founder Of 'Stand Tall'*

When I think of Derek, my heart melts. This man is an exceptional human being, not only because he is a professional surfer who is blind, but also his character and integrity touch me. He truly is a great friend.

Derek, more than any person I have ever met, faces hardship and difficulties with the most positive, joyful attitude. I hardly ever see him without a smile on his face and nothing is impossible for him. Absolutely nothing!

I have known Derek Rabelo for five years. I first met him in Sydney at our 'Stand Tall' event for high school students. Angie Farr-Jones, Ros

TESTIMONIALS

Hills and I started this charity in 2013. 'Stand Tall' is designed to build hope into the lives of young people. We bring high profile young role models such as sports men and women, community workers and we have even had a former drug dealer to speak to young people to inspire and motivate them for their lifelong journey.

Derek adores his mother, she came out to Australia in October 2015 and she was so delighted to watch Derek speak at the 'Stand Tall' event. Some friends of Derek asked her to share her story, as they were so impressed with her story in the 'Beyond Sight' movie. She gave her story through an interpreter.

She explained that she was heartbroken when Derek was born blind. She said that every day she asked God to heal her son for the first ten years – crying every night. She also prayed every day, asking God to show her how to raise this little blind boy. When he turned 10 years old, her tears stopped. God told her to stop crying and she understood that Derek had a special purpose. After that, she just enjoyed the way Derek was. She has been an incredible influence in Derek's life a guiding influence in his very strong Christian faith. She continues to pray for him every day, especially now that he is facing some of the largest, most dangerous waves around the world.

I have never met anybody who totally trusts God as much as Derek does. People are absolutely amazed that he knows when to get on a wave because God tells him. He can tell you when every wave is coming. He can hear a wave. He will say to people on the shore, "Get back, there is a big wave coming."

Derek has the best sense of humour. He will say things like, 'Sorry I didn't see you' if he cuts in front of another surfer. He makes fun of catching huge waves because he says he can't be frightened of what he can't see. He has an incredible gift to discern people's motives and character. If a friend has a new girlfriend, he will introduce her to Derek, and Derek just seems to know whether or not she is right for him.

Derek is also extremely generous. When he speaks at a school or event, he is happy to spend hours having 'selfies' taken with them. Derek smiles with each child, making them all feel valued and important. In 2013, Derek spoke to a full assembly at St Lukes Grammar in Sydney. There was a young man in Year 7 in the assembly who had a disease that was making him go blind. Derek was introduced to this young man to have a photo taken with him. Derek spent a lot of time with this boy and he followed up with phone calls to him. The boy came along to the showing of the 'Beyond Sight' movie with his father. This encouraged the boy and his father so much. He was so grateful and made to feel incredibly special.

Derek has an indomitable spirit, joy and positivity. He is very caring about other people, always asking about family and friends. He is very aware of other peoples' needs.

LYNETTE MONROE *Family friend*

Derek is very dear to me and my family also loves him. He just has a way with him that endears you to him. He has a childlike manner, but at the same time he is highly intelligent.

I had met Derek at the first premiere of his movie. I took my three boys and we all met Derek after the showing, which was very exciting for all of us. This was in my hometown of San Clemente, Southern California. That was my initiation into meeting this legend.

A year later, I received a call from the church saying they were looking for a few host families to host Derek Rabelo and were we interested?

Because we were a surfing family, we were asked if we would like to host him for a couple of weeks, as he was going to be here throughout the whole summer. I said I would like to have him for a month, but I had to call Scott, my husband, to run it past him. He was unsure because Derek had a big following and he was filming movies at the time. He said, "How about a few weeks?"

I wanted my family to see how it is to live with a man who cannot see and lives his life with such great faith. I felt this would be good for our family to experience this." I have three boys and Derek was still just a boy, so I thought it would be a great idea.

Scott agreed to host Derek for a month. Honestly, we weren't sure what to expect. Within a week of moving in, Derek had our entire floor planned out. He knew where everything was. He fitted in with our family so well. The boys adored him and they loved taking him surfing. We quickly realized that hosting him and giving him a place to live was really not what it was about. It was our family embracing him and having our lives changed. I felt that he was like a son to me. I would get on skype or Facetime with Lia his mother and I would tell her I would take care of her baby. We would all take care of him. She was so grateful for that.

I wondered if I was going to have to drive this boy around. They said he had a driver and a friend helping him and his name was Caio. We all fell in love with Derek and Caio. Caio stayed with us as well, although he didn't speak any English. But he was really homesick and went back to Brazil.

The month was coming to an end and Scott said, "I just love Derek, he should just stay here for the rest of the summer – for as long as he wants." But he was scheduled to also live with other families. Derek didn't want to go anywhere else. We didn't want him to go away, but he was traveling to Brazil, Australia and Indonesia.

Scott and I met Derek in Indonesia on a surfing holiday. Well, the two guys surfed, not me! Derek was on the back of the scooter, which everyone rides there and he was barely hanging on. He was so relaxed. My heart was on my sleeve. The guys surfed every day. One day, Derek hung out with me on a giant rock called Uluratu. We were sitting watching guys surfing. I would explain to him what I was seeing, explaining to him what the surfers were doing. Derek just wanted to hear from me how the waves looked and their shape. We talked about clouds. He didn't understand clouds, so I told him clouds were like marshmallows. It was such a special time.

I remember the first time I sent him off in an Uber by himself. I was in awe; this blind boy was going to the airport with his surfboard. When he came back home to us after a long trip to Indonesia, he was so sick. He walked in my door, barely even put his bags down and collapsed on my couch and said, "I'm home." I gave him some hot tea and medicine. We nursed him back to health. It is such a compliment that someone wants to be with you.

Derek would ride up and down the street on a bike or skateboard or anything, just cruising in the street. All the neighborhood kids fell in love with him. Derek's father, Ernesto, came and stayed with us for a few weeks. Then he and Derek did another trip to Indonesia. We got on so well with Ernesto, and he absolutely adores his son and they joke about everything.

Derek told us about meeting Maddy, the love of his life, and we were so excited. Soon after we got the call from Derek saying that he was going to propose to Maddy. Literally two days later, they called us to say they were engaged. Derek wanted us to be at the wedding and Scott to be in the wedding party. I was so excited for him and Maddy seemed like such a lovely girl. Derek was so happy. However, we hadn't met Maddy, only Facetimed her occasionally.

We had a great time at Margaret River in Western Australia where the wedding was held.

After they got married they lived with us for a while until they found their apartment. Derek didn't need me so much then, as he had a wife of his own. I just love the fact that we have Derek in our lives. It has been a very special experience for us.

SCOTT MONROE *Family friend*

I first heard about Derek through the movie 'Beyond Sight.' The following year he was coming out to America to promote the movie and when I told some of my friends we were looking after Derek, everybody thought that was nice, but said, "He's not going to end up staying." Everyone has the impression he is a famous person. I must admit, I felt the same way.

When Derek stayed with us, I knew he was just a young kid who was excited about his life and he had a great sense of humor. He was just like any other 20-year-old kid. I related well to him. It made me want to help him and take him surfing, although he is half my age. But age isn't important to him. He was very genuine, approachable and easy to talk to, easy to laugh with... Always playing a practical joke.

But if you get to know him, he has no limitations at all. When he did get married he came back to us. I do remember sharing some things with Derek. I said, "You are growing up really fast. You have a wife to care for - you have a family. You need to look to the future. You can do anything – but what are you going to do?"

Many Brazilians live for today. They just celebrate the moment. I tried to help him to look to the future as he's not a sponsored surfer anymore. Derek is an authentic person. He connects in relationships, is a believer in the Word and has so much faith. He believes the best in people and circumstances. One great thing is that he dreams big.

Derek has no fear in anything – in relationships, new adventures, or trying something brand new, including downhill skiing. Derek just wants to go faster. That is his motivation; that is how he is wired.

MAGNO OLIVEIRA *Family friend*

Derek and I are from the same town in Brazil – Guarapari. In this town we have 120,000 people living there. It is quite small. One beach where everyone goes to surf is called Praia Do Marro, which is close to me. This is the most famous beach for waves. I started to hear about Derek from everyone on the beach, but I had never seen him before. People would say, "Did you meet this blind guy?" I had been hearing some great stories about him.

Finally, we were surfing at the same time and I met him. We started talking from there. I said, "Whenever you want to surf, let me know I can help you." Derek wanted to come into my world. Everyone was saying I was crazy because of my love of big waves. Derek was very open to experiencing new waves. He was very bored quite often so he wanted to go to the next level. So I was the best guy because I was looking for the biggest waves.

Derek would call me every morning asking how the surf was. I said, "I don't know whether I can take you."

Derek would say, "I want to go where you are going." He wanted the types of waves I was surfing as a body-boarder. Not many surfers like to go on a surfboard and ride waves that body-boarders like.

I was taking him to these crazy waves that even my pro surfer friends wouldn't surf. Many were telling me I was going to kill Derek or end his career. They all thought they were risking their own lives. I always told Derek I wouldn't take him, but he would be upset with me, so I had to take him. He was so determined.

ROBSON ALVES DO AMARAL *Family friend*

I met Derek at the end of 2006 when he was 13 or 14 years old. I had just bought an apartment in the building where he lived and did not know the city well. On leaving for lunch, he was at the building's concierge and as I was new to the area, I started chatting and asked about restaurants nearby. He suggested a spot, giving details of the type of food and precise directions on how to get there. I had seen him walking around, but I did not know he lived there.

Later, I talked to him again and we agreed to have lunch together the next day in another place he knew. I was impressed by his knowledge of the area, his sense of direction and his detailed description of the route, but what especially caught my attention was his palate for food. I named him my 'personal gourmet guide,' a title he still holds to this day.

We talked more often and I met his parents and knew the ranch of his grandmother Cleusa, where I noticed his interest and affection for family, nature and animals.

Gradually I was observing his independence and ability to move around and relate to people and the environment. He had a healthy curiosity about everything. The development of his various senses (he has several other senses beyond hearing, touch, taste and smell) is something that impresses those who know him. Quick reasoning, extraordinary memory, an unusual and natural gentleness in dealing with people associated with a fine and intelligent good mood make him a human being above average. He's a people charmer!

I have a special admiration for his firmness of character, his remarkable personality and his common sense in all the decisions he makes concerning his course and for those around him. I see there the good fruits of the seeds planted by his parents and family in his education.

His success in sports is what catches the attention of the public, but his insatiable desire to know and do new things is part of his daily life. He has already done things that few people have done or will do during their lives.

Derek is and will be successful in any activity that he proposes, sporting or not.

ROSEMAREE KNIGHT *Retired /Sports Ministry Networker*

I have known Derek Rabelo for a number of years. For me, these have been great, inspiring and happy years. I am what is known as a 'networker,' mostly of Christian ministries, but especially sports ministries and resources. I networked my way into Derek's ministry and life – quite by accident.

As a child, my father had interested me in small texts etc. and this grew into a love of Christian Bookstores. Being single I had helped with a singles group and had friends across denominations. I joined Southern Cross Ski Lodge and then later Sports Chaplaincy Australia... this led me to volunteer in the 'Quest Australia More Than Gold' Office – for Sydney's Olympics and Paralympics & beyond from Oct 1997 to 2002. I loved this time as I met more wonderful people doing amazing things which then put me into the International Sports Ministry scene especially South Pacific and sports ministry resources for Major Events but also so much more, as hundreds of awesome people working in a variety of initiatives attended these annual conferences.

It was in one of those global meetings that I first heard about Derek. One of the session delegates came in bursting with excitement because he had been at another conference where he had seen a blind surfer.

He told us there would be a movie coming out.

Meanwhile, exciting things were happening in Australia. I was asked by two friends who knew of my networking to join meetings, which would later be called 'Stand Tall,' a great charity aimed at building hope in the lives of young Australians.

In the first three years there were many challenges, so I suggested to the two leaders, "What about the blind surfer?" Derek and Bryan Jennings agreed to bring the movie to Australia with many edits yet to be done.

It was all very amazing, as none of us had ever met Bryan and Derek. Derek had to fly from Brazil to meet up with Bryan, then together they came... Such a long way for a young man who couldn't see to meet people he didn't know. Travel expenses were paid for by Jake Betlam from C3 Church, which was also very remarkable, as they didn't know him either.

Derek had very little English at that stage. Now he loves to joke and have fun. People grossly underestimate him... he is very switched on and clever/smart. That visit was an amazing time for us all. Friendships were formed. We were all so blessed that God had brought them to our shores.

Derek reads people extremely well. He also is caring of people of all ages. He really loves people and loves to meet new people. He does endless 'selfies' with people - they cue up to be photographed with him.

Derek doesn't want people to treat him as disabled. People, when they first see him, think that because he is blind he has to sit down! In reality, people don't need to look after him.

Derek is inspiring. He is not afraid to go anywhere or do anything. It doesn't matter if he knows people or not – he will even go to places where he doesn't know anyone. He is prepared to step out into the unknown.

Derek can assess people's feelings. To Derek, life is an adventure. People are drawn to him, people of all ages. He loves to invite people to church and quickly offers to pray if they tell him of a problem.

Derek and I did a trip to New Zealand, which was interesting. To my surprise, Derek went surfing in the freezing cold water. He really impacted the children, especially disabled kids. Two people have been remarkable in caring for Derek. Bryan Jennings took him under his wing, taught him English, introduced him to sports ministry, produced a movie on his life and took him traveling. And Jeanine Treharne is so remarkable in her care for Derek, pouring a great deal of love on him as if he belonged to their family and taking care of many details. He has been blessed to be a blessing…

REV MARGARET COURT AO, MBE *Former professional Tennis Player and Senior Minister, Victory Life*

I met Derek Rabello when he came to speak at our CityWide youth group. I was impacted by his story, his humility and his strength of character and his obvious trust in and love for God.

Derek was a warm and friendly personality. Nothing seemed to offend or upset him and he certainly carried an 'air' about him that nothing was impossible for him and that he hadn't let his lack of natural vision define what he could or couldn't do.

Derek attended our Victory Life International Bible Training School for a few months and was an inspiration to the international and local students and would challenge and encourage them to follow their dreams and have a vision for their future. He was truly an inspiration to others who thought they had some type of handicap and disability.

It was during his time at the Bible School that he made a connection with a German student called Madeline Kunert. The strong friendship they developed grew into a love story and they ended up being married by our worship Pastor, Ps Rob Scott, and as was fitting, they married on the famous surfing beach of Margaret River.

This was truly a great love story as Derek was from Brazil, Madeline from Germany and they found each other in the most isolated city in the world – Perth, Western Australia.

I wish him great success with this book and pray that it will truly inspire others that nothing is impossible when you trust and lean on the Spirit of God and your love for Jesus.

I know Derek will be such an inspiration to many young people in the world.

CONTACT DEREK RABELO VIA

WWW.DEREKRABELO.COM

ABOUT THE AUTHOR

Lynn Goldsmith resides on the Northern Beaches in Sydney, Australia. She was introduced to Derek Rabelo and entrusted with writing his amazing story.

Lynn is an Editor and Journalist. She was previously Editor in Chief for a number of magazines and is the author of five published books.

To get in contact with Lynn direct, email her on lynngoldsmith194@gmail.com.

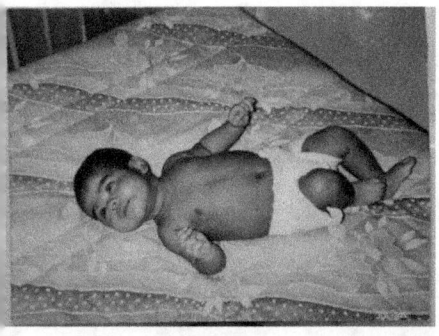
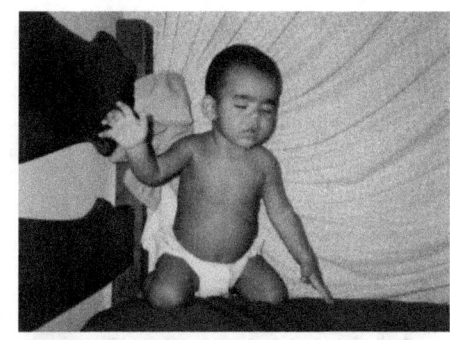

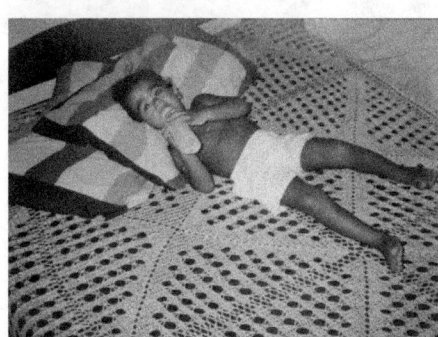
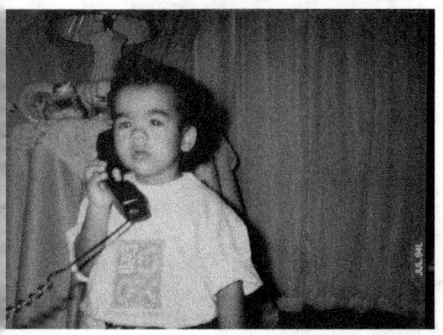
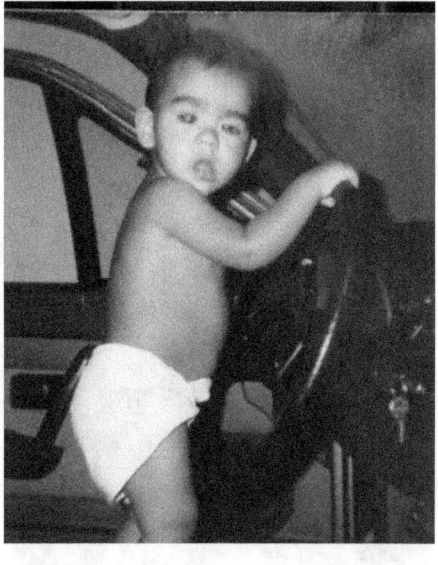

Derek as a baby.

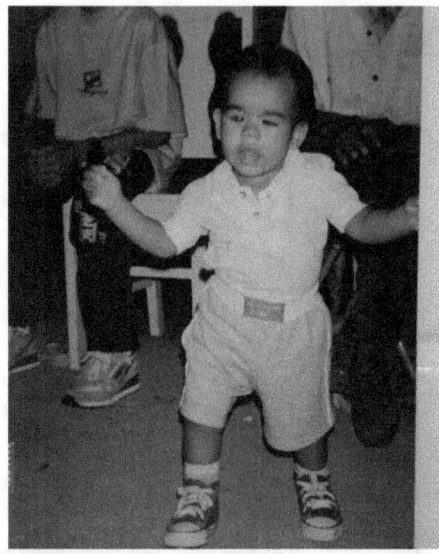

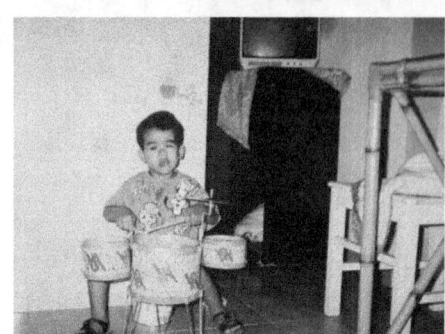

Derek as an energetic young boy.

Derek and his father Ernesto looking for adventures.

Above: Derek living life to the fullest at a young age. Below: Derek's surfing career begins…

Clockwise from top: Derek at Pipeline; Claudio and Derek; (images courtesy Bruno Lemos); Team Arpoador; Derek at sunset.

Clockwise from top: Derek being towed in by Carlos Burle; Ricardo Arona, Nick Bevan and Derek at Moskova Gym; Gabriel Pensador blindfolded with Derek; Legend surfer Derek Ho with Derek (who he was named after).

Clockwise from top: Derek surfing at Rock Piles (Dec 2012); Derek and his father Ernesto at the Olympics; Derek with Kelly Slater; Derek at the WCT in Rio 2013.

Clockwise from top left: Derek conquering another extreme sport; Maddy and Derek on their wedding day; Derek, Maddy and Serenity; Family friends.

www.ingramcontent.com/pod-product-compliance
Lightning Source LLC
LaVergne TN
LVHW051516070426
835507LV00023B/3148